I mended page

DATE DUE		
JUL 2 7 2012		
AUG 0 7 2012		

知識漫畫版
（中英對照）

認識台灣歷史
A HISTORY OF TAIWAN IN COMICS

● 總策劃〉吳密察　　● 漫畫繪製〉朱鴻琦、葉銍桐　　● 劇本編寫〉陳婉箐
● 英文版策劃〉文魯彬（Robin J. Winkler）
● 英文審訂〉翁佳音、賴慈芸、耿柏瑞（Brian A. Kennedy）
● 英文翻譯〉白啟賢（Matthew Clarke）

4 清朝時代（上）：唐山過台灣
The Cing Dynasty (I):
Leaving the Mainland for Taiwan

新自然主義股份有限公司　出版

目錄

打開台灣歷史大門

小野
（知名專業作家）

台灣人越來越有信心了，
這些信心不再只是靠經濟奇蹟或政治奇蹟，
而是靠自我認同，認同自己的歷史，
認同自己的身世。
我想我會推薦這本書給我的孩子閱讀，
讓他們認同自己的身世
進而認同自己，不再自卑。

巴札克・吉靈
（台灣民主基金會主任）

當台灣逐漸民主化、多元化的今天，
我們欣喜見到人們開始願意更敞開心胸去面對
發生在這塊土地上真實的過去，
並且為未來新而完整的文化藍圖而努力。
至少這部《認識台灣歷史》讓我們看到了這樣的過程，
而且新自然主義公司洪發行人的用心及
台大歷史系吳密察老師的精研，
更令人感到佩服。

呂秀菊
（全國教師會理事長）

歷史是一個耐人尋味的故事，
也是一面鏡子。
《認識台灣歷史》從關懷出發，
走過先人的足跡，啟迪後人之智慧，
寓教於畫，格外深刻動人。

李遠哲
（中央研究院院長）

恭喜貴出版社製作完成這一套
形式與風格別具特色的台灣史書籍，
我相信在今天影像圖案與文字結合出版
特別講究的時代，這一套書對台灣的中小學生
認識自己生長的土地與社會，
必有相當大的助益。

林玉体
（台灣師範大學教育學系教授、
考試院考試委員）

《認識台灣歷史》好看又翔實，
請大家趕快來看。

城仲模
（司法院副院長）

用漫畫方式提綱挈領，
細膩分說台灣縱橫四百年史，
可謂為深入淺出，老少咸宜，
並能向上提昇作為有格調、有尊嚴的
台灣人的一部絕佳參考自修的
簡明台灣史書。

夏鑄九
（台灣大學建築與城鄉研究所教授）

這是早在我們的童年
就該看到的漫畫！

馬英九
（台北市市長）

這是一套可愛、可敬、又可讀的書。
它與八十年前連雅堂先生的《台灣通史》
雖然創作於不同的年代，採用不同的
表現方式，卻有一貫的關懷與反省。
特別的是，
這套書將趣味與嚴肅巧妙的結合在一起，
創作者及出版者的用心與努力，
都值得我們喝采。

陳水扁

（總統）

我一直認為，我們讀歷史，不僅是知道
過去做了什麼，更重要的是，我們未來要怎麼做？
然而歷史作為一種紀錄，也無可避免的受到
撰寫人本身思維或觀點的影響，而左右歷史呈現的面向。
台灣史也是如此，過去我們在求學時期，
其實並沒有完整的台灣史教學，甚至獨立的台灣史讀本，
歷史課本裡有關台灣的部分並不多，而且並非
是以台灣為主體的描述，因此大家對於台灣的歷史往往難窺全貌，
影響所及就是大家對台灣的國家定位認識不清，
今天許多爭議亦由此產生。
所以對於這套以台灣為論述主體的台灣史，
尤其是以漫畫形態表達，更是深入淺出、彌足珍貴，
對於台灣史的教育可說貢獻良多。

黃武雄

（台灣大學數學系教授）

這是一套很有啟發性的漫畫書，
大人與孩子都會喜歡看。對於大人：當作消遣，
躺在床上看了一遍，便會對台灣歷史有了整體的概念。
歷史是人類共同的記憶，台灣語族目前面臨的
兩個危機是失語病與失憶症，透過閱讀一套漫畫書，
我們能多少拾回失去的記憶。
對於孩子：看這一套漫畫，是個開始，
讓他所傳承的文化與歷史在他心中萌芽，
讓他免於記憶斷裂的挫折，
成長為一個意識健康的人。

謝長廷
（高雄市市長）

《認識台灣歷史》是一個重大的突破。
它跳脫傳統歷史學者寫作方式，
用淺顯易懂的漫畫，深入淺出呈現台灣歷史的真相。
期盼藉由這套書的發行，能引起社會大眾的共鳴，
認真思考台灣永續發展的問題。

蕭新煌
（中央研究院社會學研究所研究員）

這是一本作為台灣人
不可不知的台灣史通俗漫畫版，
老少咸宜。讀台灣史，想台灣未來，
這是很好的入門漫畫集。

龔鵬程
（佛光人文社會學院文學研究所教授）

研究歷史，可以通古今之變；
了解歷史，可以幫助我們認識自己。
《認識台灣歷史》具有這兩方面的功能，
且簡明扼要，生動有趣，
非常適合社會一般人士閱讀，
新自然主義公司在
策劃、編輯、繪製、考證、撰寫的用心，
頗堪推許。

藍順德
（國立編譯館館長）

漫畫的魅力十足，
是成長過程中不可或缺的良師益友。
《認識台灣歷史》透過
生動、活潑、有趣的圖畫及故事，
可引領孩子了解自己所生長的這塊土地，
更能體會先人蓽路藍縷
開拓台灣的精神。

（依姓名筆畫排列）

期待一部淺顯易懂、均衡適中的台灣史

吳密察（本書總策劃，台灣大學歷史系副教授）

　　一部深入淺出、均衡適中的歷史書，必須建立在堅實豐富的研究基礎之上，而且也必須脫離長期以來政治因素過度干涉的思想偏執。

　　這部《認識台灣歷史》試圖跳開各種成見，並充分吸收晚近的研究成果，重新勾繪台灣史的圖像。但是，當工作開始之後所遇到的困難，卻遠比預期的多。這些困難，有些是來自於必須將生硬的學院派體裁之研究成果，轉變成生動、有趣之讀物（即「戲劇化」）的過程；有些則是因為傳統歷史家大多只根據文字資料重建歷史，而且也只以文字表述歷史，但一部漫畫版台灣史則必須將歷史「視覺化」。在「戲劇化」、「視覺化」的雙重要求下，就必須要兼顧「寫實」與「示意」。這的確是一項艱鉅的工作。

　　《認識台灣歷史》雖然以淺顯的形式敘述歷史，但其中蘊含著對台灣這塊我們生活的土地及人民深厚的關愛，對台灣「如何走過來」之歷史的溫情與反省，甚至也希望對台灣的歷史教育發出改革的訊息。希望這些用心都能因讀者的耐心，點點滴滴得到共鳴。那麼，做為這部《認識台灣歷史》的企劃、監修者，將會非常高興。

老少咸宜的台灣歷史書

　　看漫畫學歷史，好看又印象深刻！《認識台灣歷史》中英對照版（十冊雙語漫畫和一冊英文版《台灣歷史小百科‧年表》），活潑生動、淺顯易讀，相信能帶領大家從歷史中得到樂趣，從樂趣中了解歷史。

　　這套簡明版的台灣歷史書，有編繪者的用心經營，請在翻閱時留意：

　　1. 本套書的陳述方式，以嘗試重現歷史、開放式思考為目標，力求做到：

　　　（1）中性用語，略微加入輕鬆鏡頭，增添閱讀趣味。

　　　（2）事實陳述，盡量不做價值判斷，讓讀者在史實進行中有所體會。

　　　（3）破除傳統偶像式迷思、揚善不隱惡，忠於可考證的史料。

　　　（4）對於通俗爭議，不提供標準化答案，由讀者於各種說法中自行研判。

　　2. 目前台灣的居民（Taiwanese），可以大別為「華人（Chinese）」和「原住民（Indigenous People）」。

　　　（1）「華人」包括二十世紀之前移入的福佬系、客家系，甚至二十世紀中期之後移入的「外省人」；一般常稱為「漢人（Han Chinese）」，本套書改稱「華人」。

　　　（2）一九九四年政府回應「原住民」的「正名」要求，不再稱「山胞」，本套書改稱「原住民」；這是個泛稱，其中因為語言、文化、社會組織等等的個別差異，還可以歸類成好幾族。

　　3. 本套書英文譯音均採行「通用拼音」；如有另一種說法，例如鄭成功之父鄭芝龍譯音為「Jheng Jhihlong」，但他在國外文獻上多以「Nicolas Iquan Cheng」出現，便在第二冊首次出現時，以欄外註的方式註明供參考；例外情況為台灣各縣市名、當代人名等等，則參考內政部公布的地名譯寫原則、政府年鑑、國際慣例、學術常用字等等拼注方式。

　　4. 英文版《台灣歷史小百科‧年表》，將十冊漫畫的精采導讀、小百科、年表、常識問答都翻成了英文，獨立成書以饗海內外讀者。

充滿無限生機的新天地

吳密察（本書總策劃，台灣大學歷史系副教授）

　　清帝國以大軍屈服了鄭氏在台灣的勢力之後，並不積極要把台灣納入版圖。對清朝政府來說，重要的是消滅了一個反抗勢力，但是對於要將一海之隔，而且同為紅毛、倭寇、海盜所窩占的台灣納入統治，卻相當消極。所以多數朝廷官員主張遷民墟地，將已來到台灣的華人遣回大陸。

　　但是施琅卻不同意這種看法。施琅出身閩南，早年也是出洋下海通販之徒，他深知閩南人必定千方百計向外謀求發展，而台灣具有各種優越條件，必定會是大家趨之若鶩的目標；而且如果不將台灣納入版圖，西洋各國也將會據之以招致華人前來貿易，那麼台灣也將成為中國東南沿海的隱憂；所以積極主張應將台灣收入版圖。最後清朝政府終於採納施琅的看法，將台灣納入版圖，設台灣府，置於福建省之下。

台灣納入大清版圖

　　清帝國雖然將台灣納入版圖，但政府最關心的是勿使台灣成為「逋逃的淵籔」，反政府的巢穴，所以在制度上設了很多防範的措施。首先，在台灣「編查流寓」，進行戶口登錄，而且將無家室、田產者遣返大陸；自大陸來台也必須申請渡航許可，透過這種出入

境管理篩檢危險份子；即使被允許來台灣，也不許攜帶家眷，這種規定具有使家眷留在大陸當人質的意味。

清朝政府不但管制大陸人來台，也不歡迎來到台灣的華人積極擴大開墾空間，那是因為惟恐華人進入台灣山區無法掌控，而且也怕華人侵入山區將造成原住民的反撲。所以清朝政府在台灣西部平原地帶的東緣設計了一道境界線，禁止華人越出開墾。因此雖說清帝國將台灣納入版圖，但其統治仍僅限於西部。

清朝政府為防範台灣人反抗，自中國大陸派遣軍隊來台駐紮。但又惟恐這些在台軍隊鞭長莫及，不聽中央號令，因此在軍制上頗費周章。在台軍隊以自大陸之不同營伍抽調部分人員組成，來到台灣後也分散駐防，並且三年一換，為的是使軍隊不能坐大和在地生根。清朝政府也不准在台募兵，怕台灣人當兵會使將帥無法約束。

前仆後繼渡台

雖然清朝政府的態度消極，但閩南、粵東的居民，卻一方面迫於內地生計困難，一方面垂涎台灣豐厚的生產條件，而蜂擁來台。台灣的土壤、氣候、水文都極適合當時最主要的農業生產。例如，清朝地方官便盛讚台灣：「土地肥沃、不糞種，糞則穗重而仆。種植後聽其自生，惟享坐穫，每每數倍內地。」即使不是來台耕種，也有甚多工作

機會：「漳泉內地無籍之民，無可耕之田，無可傭之工，無可覓之食，一到台地，上可致富，下可溫飽。一切農工商賈以至百藝之末，計工授值，比之內地，率皆倍蓰。」

　　但是，積極想渡海來台追求更好生活的閩南、粵東人士，卻未必都能獲得政府批准來台，因此只好以各種非法方法，例如買通守口官員私放，假冒漁民矇混出海，甚至由「人蛇」安排偷渡。偷渡來台的過程中，或者三番兩次被不肖之徒所騙，或者喪身海底，甚至已來到台灣又被官府捕獲強制遣返，歷經辛酸。所以，雖然「台灣錢淹腳目」，但「唐山過台灣，心肝結歸丸」。

第1章
施琅與
「台灣棄留疏」

Bringing Taiwan into the
Cing Empire:
Admiral Shih Lang and His Report
on Taiwan

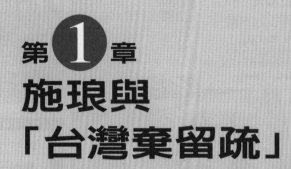

一六八二年，清朝
政府命福建水師提
督施琅征討台灣。

In 1682, the Cing
Government ordered
Fujian Admiral Shih Lang
to overtake Taiwan.

隔年六月，施琅率
戰船三百艘、兵力
二萬專征台灣。

In June 1683, Shih led
an attack force of 300
warships and 20,000
soldiers into Taiwan.

施琅原是鄭成功手下大將，後來因鄭成功殺其父、弟，改而投效清朝政府。

Shih had been a general under Jheng Chenggong, the ruler of Taiwan. But when Jheng Chenggong executed Shih's father and younger brother, Shih left the Jheng clan forces and joined their enemy, the Cing Government.

這一天終於來了。
The day has finally come.

施琅
Shih Lang

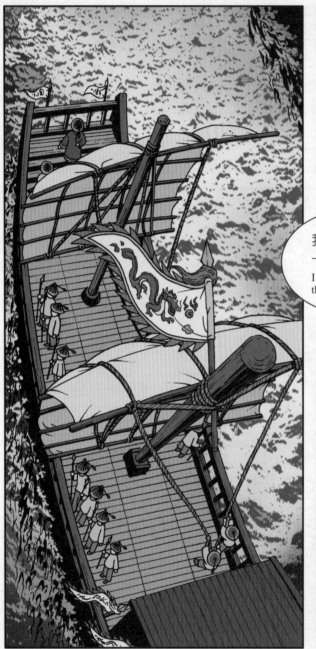

我永遠記得那一天。
I'll never forget that day.

刀下留人。
Hold the execution!

施琅之父
Shih Lang's Father

施琅之弟
Shih Lang's Brother

施琅！
Shih Lang!

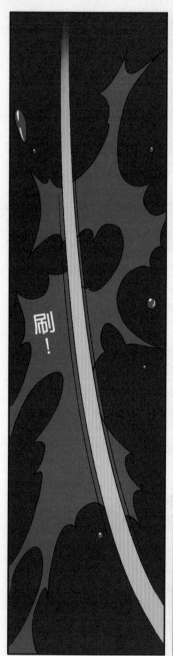

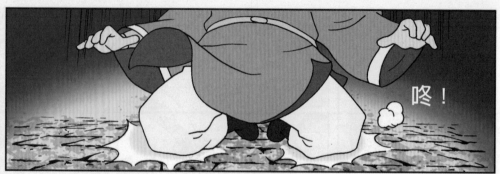

報仇心切的施琅，終於等到機會率兵攻台。他的戰略是先拿下澎湖。

Burning with a desire for revenge, Shih finally got the chance to lead the attack on Taiwan. His strategy was to take the Penghu Islands first.

鄭軍在失去澎湖後人心大亂，鄭克塽決定投降，施琅入台接受歸誠，鄭氏王朝畫下句點。

Shih's victory at Penghu threw Jheng's forces into chaos. In the end, Jheng Chenggong's grandson, Jheng Keshuang, surrendered and Shih took control of the island. The Jheng clan's reign over Taiwan had come to an end.

踏上台灣土地的施琅，察覺台灣是個蘊藏無限生機的地方。

Shih soon recognized that Taiwan held infinite potential for development.

這裡土地還真是肥沃，
與內地的江南地區相比，
絲毫不遜色。

This land is really fertile. It holds
its own with any of the lands
south of the Yangtze River.

大人，台灣
好地方可多
得很呢！

Taiwan is full of
rich land.

哦！

Hmm.

出城看看，您就知
道原因了。

When we start exploring,
you'll see what I mean.

那還等什麼，
快帶路吧！

What are we
waiting for?
Lead the way!

施琅征服台灣的消息，立刻快馬加鞭回報給清朝皇帝知道。

Word that Shih had taken Taiwan quickly reached the Cing emperor.

啪！

中國北京・紫禁城
The Forbidden City, Beijing

哈！哈！
Ha, ha!

真不愧是鄭成功以前的手下大將，三兩下就把在台灣的逆賊收服了。

Just what I expected from a former general under Jheng Chenggong. Taking back Taiwan from the rebels was like a walk in the park for Shih.

康熙皇帝
Emperor Kangsi

施提督的確神勇無比，消除了海疆之患，不知皇上打算如何處理台灣？

Shih is definitely a hero, but now that he's defeated the rebels on Taiwan, what does Your Majesty intend to do with the island?

這⋯⋯

Yes, well ... hmm.

把鄭氏逆賊全部押回審理。

Bring all the Jheng clan rebels back to be tried.

只不過是個小島，何必想這麼多？

I can't believe we're wracking our brains thinking about what to do with a little island.

皇上可別忘了那台灣小島上還有不少人呢！

Your Majesty, don't forget that a lot of people other than the Jhengs live on Taiwan.

是啊，要如何處理那些人呢？

That's true. What are we going to do with them?

......
......

眾卿有何見解？

What do you gentlemen think?

啓奏皇上，台灣只是個小島，且又隔著海峽，若要納入版圖，勢必得派人管理，如此大費周章，恐將浪費國帑。

Your Majesty, as you say, Taiwan is just a small island across the strait. To bring it into the empire, we'd have to send officials to govern it. The time and effort involved would be a waste of our empire's resources.

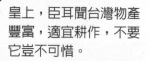

不如將那裡的人全部遷回內地就是了。

Just bring them all back to the mainland.

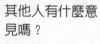

其他人有什麼意見嗎？

Any other opinions?

皇上，臣耳聞台灣物產豐富，適宜耕作，不要它豈不可惜。

Your Majesty, I've heard that Taiwan has abundant natural resources and is highly suited for agriculture. Wouldn't it be a shame to give up such a place?

我大清地大物博，小小台灣有何可惜！

The great Cing Empire has land and resources to spare. What do we need tiny Taiwan for?

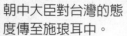

朝中大臣對台灣的態度傳至施琅耳中。

When Shih Lang heard of the Imperial Court's attitude toward Taiwan, he was furious.

京城那些人腦袋都壞了嗎？居然想放棄一座海上仙島。

Have the people in the capital lost their minds! How can they let a jewel like Taiwan slip through their fingers?

豈有此理！
How ridiculous!

看來我不出馬是不行的。

Looks like I've got to take action.

施琅知道台灣的好處，堅持主張將台灣收入版圖，於是向康熙皇帝提出「台灣棄留疏」，分析棄留台灣之利弊得失。

Shih Lang knew what Taiwan had to offer. Hoping to change the Imperial Court's thinking about Taiwan, he wrote a report for the emperor titled "On the Territorialization of Taiwan". In it Shih described how the benefits of bringing Taiwan into the Cing Empire far outweighed the drawbacks.

台灣地理位置四通八達，舟楫往來頻繁，是東南江浙閩粵四省的屏障……

Taiwan's location is excellent. The island is accessible from all sides; ships come and go regularly. Taiwan is the barrier that stands between the outside world and Jiangsu, Jhejiang, Fujian and Guangdong provinces.

這裡物產豐富，舉凡硫磺、鹿皮、糖蔗等無所不有。

Taiwan has a wide variety of abundant natural resources: deer hides, sugar cane, sulfur, etc. It wants for nothing.

完成了。
Finished.

施琅為了說服康熙皇帝而上奏的「台灣棄留疏」，帶給台灣命運空前的影響，是他當初始料未及的。

Shih had high hopes that "On the Territorialization of Taiwan" would change the emperor's mind about Taiwan, but he never expected that this document would have an unprecedented impact on Taiwan's future.

太子少保、靖海將軍、靖海侯兼管福建水師提督事務臣施琅謹題，為恭陳台灣棄留之利害，仰祈睿裁事。

竊照台灣地方，北連吳會，南接粵嶠，延袤數千里，山川峻峭，港道迂迴，乃江、浙、閩、粵四省之左護；隔離澎湖一峽，水道三更餘遙。查明季大洋，水道三更餘遙。查明季設水澎標於金門所，出汛至澎湖而止，水道亦有七更餘遙。

台灣一地，原屬化外，土番雜處，未入版圖也。然其時中國之民潛至、生聚於其間者，已不下萬人。鄭芝龍為海寇時，以為巢穴。及崇禎元年，鄭芝龍就撫，將此地稅與紅毛為互市之所。紅毛遂聯絡土番，招納內地人民，成一海外之國，漸作邊患……

30

台灣居民多已在其地安定下來，現在要他們遷回，恐有擾民之虞。

Many of the people living in Taiwan are already quite settled there. If you asked them to leave, I think they would be very upset.

為了天下安定，犧牲一些人是在所難免的。

The sacrifice of a few is a small price to pay for the safety and stability of the empire.

但是，就算要遷回內地，也需要很長一段時間，而且又無法確定是否有人被遺漏。

But it would take a very long time to move all the residents back to the mainland. Furthermore, we would have no way of knowing whether or not anyone had escaped or been left behind.

即使遺漏，也僅僅是少數，不足為患。

Even if a few little fishes managed to escape the net, they wouldn't present a danger.

說得有理。
Indeed, indeed.

沒錯！
True, true.

32

諸位別忘了台灣還有番人，若是那些漏網之魚，潛入深山溪谷中，勾結番人，再加上因犯罪而逃往台灣的人及士兵，一旦狗急跳牆，變成海盜，必然會騷擾沿海居民。

Don't forget about the savages. What if those left behind entered the mountains and colluded with the savages? And what if this group was joined by escaped criminals and soldiers? We would have a dangerous band of pirates on our hands harassing the coastal people.

海盜並非起於一朝一夕，現在就已經很多了。

What's the difference? There are already plenty of pirates around.

還有更糟的嗎？

Is there something worse?

海盜事小，我擔心的是……

Actually, pirates are a small matter. What I'm really worried about is ...

註：本書人物對話部分，為符合故事所設定情境，「原住民」一詞將適時改稱「番人」或「番仔」。
NOTE: To reflect the usage of the times, the term "savages" has been used in place of the contemporary term "indigenous peoples."

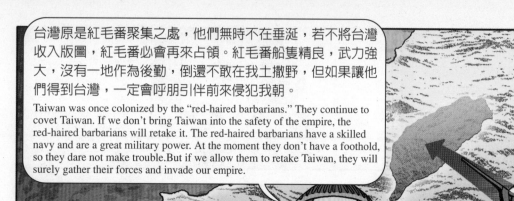

台灣原是紅毛番聚集之處，他們無時不在垂涎，若不將台灣收入版圖，紅毛番必會再來占領。紅毛番船隻精良，武力強大，沒有一地作為後勤，倒還不敢在我土撒野，但如果讓他們得到台灣，一定會呼朋引伴前來侵犯我朝。

Taiwan was once colonized by the "red-haired barbarians." They continue to covet Taiwan. If we don't bring Taiwan into the safety of the empire, the red-haired barbarians will retake it. The red-haired barbarians have a skilled navy and are a great military power. At the moment they don't have a foothold, so they dare not make trouble.But if we allow them to retake Taiwan, they will surely gather their forces and invade our empire.

我們可以發動大軍，迎敵痛擊。

We can meet their attack with troops of our own.

但是亂事不斷，沿海居民將永無寧日。而且一旦要討伐在台灣的叛逆或紅毛番，又得勞師動眾，跨海遠征。大海無情，我軍恐強不過波濤。

That's no good either. There would be fighting back and forth. People on the coast would not be able to live in peace. If we went fighting with the red-haired barbarians or the rebels on Taiwan, we would have to both mobilize a large force and transport them across the sea. The forces of nature pose a great threat to our ships.

註：當時稱荷蘭人為紅毛番。

NOTE: Chinese of the period referred to the Dutch as the "red-haired barbarians".

註：「廈門」在西方文獻中多作 Amoy。
NOTE: Siamen was formerly known as Amoy.

一旦台灣成為我朝領土，派兵駐守，即使有逆賊蠢蠢欲動，也不敢太過囂張。

Once Taiwan becomes Cing territory and is garrisoned, even if someone is stupid enough to rebel, they wouldn't dare to get too out of hand.

施提督好像很有把握台灣一定會納入版圖內，台灣值得嗎？

Admiral Shih, you seem quite certain that Taiwan should be made a part of the Cing Empire. Do you believe it's worth the effort?

是啊，小小的台灣有必要徵調軍隊前往駐守嗎？

Good question. Do we really need to send troops to a little place like Taiwan?

我親身體驗過台灣之好，所以主張不要放棄台灣。至於派兵駐守一事，臣已想好無需增兵添餉之策。

I am determined to make Taiwan Cing territory because I've seen with my own eyes what an exceptional place it is. As for stationing troops, I've already thought of a way to guard Taiwan without adding one more soldier to the army.

素來內地的東南沿海因防範鄭氏，多置兵員，現在鄭氏已滅，可從中汰減，分別防守台、澎。

For a long time, troops have been stationed along the coast to protect against Jheng's forces. Now that they've been defeated, we can assign some of those troops to Taiwan and Penghu.

施提督思慮周延，但台灣遠在海外，難保駐台統領不會擁兵自重。

But Admiral Shih, Taiwan is across the sea, far away from the mainland. What's to stop the military leader from making himself the "king" of the island?

可以二至三年就轉移內地，統將不長久帶兵，就不會有擁兵自重的情形。

We could give the troops short assignments – two or three years. That way, relationships between soldiers and their generals will never get close enough to pose a threat.

嗯！果然是思慮周全，面面俱到。

You've thought of all the angles.

我只是認為一旦放棄台灣會釀成大禍，留著它反而能穩固邊疆。

I think that letting Taiwan go is asking for trouble, while adding it to the empire will make our border safe.

小小的一個台灣，居然讓大家傷透腦筋，商討許久，朕若不要它，不知哪一日又會跑出個鄭成功，就把它收入版圖吧！

This little island has given us some big headaches. After thinking it over, I've decided that we have to bring Taiwan into the Empire. If we don't, who knows when another Jheng Chenggong will appear.

由於施琅的「台灣棄留疏」，清朝政府於一六八三年（康熙二十二年），在台灣設台灣府，下轄諸羅、台灣、鳳山三縣，隸屬福建省。台灣自此正式納入中國版圖。

Because of Shih Lang's "On the Territorialization of Taiwan", the Cing Government officially annexed Taiwan in 1683. They established the prefecture of Taiwan, placed it under the administration of Fujian Province and divided it into three counties: Fongshan, Taiwan, and Jhuluo.

施琅與台南大天后宮

　　台南大天后宮被列為國家一級古蹟，它的歷史要從鄭氏時代說起。鄭經掌權後，邀請明朝的宗室寧靖王來台定居，並為他在當時的台江海岸邊建造了富麗宏偉的「寧靖王府」。鄭氏投降清朝，寧靖王自殺，施琅隨即進駐此地，並向清朝政府建議將此地改建為媽祖廟，這是一方面要消除明朝的精神象徵，另一方面則因施琅說他的攻台軍隊因媽祖幫助而得勝，所以要感謝媽祖（其實也是怕清朝政府猜忌）。廟名原叫「大天妃宮」，後來因為媽祖被朝封為「天后」，就改叫「大天后宮」。

　　今日，大家可以在大天后宮內看見一塊台灣島內最古老的清代石碑，這是一六八三年（康熙二十二年）施琅所立的「平台紀略碑」，其中記載施琅「平定」台灣的經過、如何安撫民心，以及經過此戰後他做的各項處置。旁邊還有一塊「功德碑」，則是一六九三年地方百姓紀念施琅的種種功績，為他立的石碑，可見施琅在當時的顯赫，與一般民間故事留給人的印象有很大的不同。

台南大天后宮已列為國家一級古蹟。（照片提供：台南大天后宮）

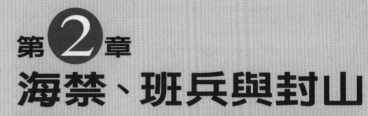

第 2 章
海禁、班兵與封山

Prohibitions and Precautions:
Cing Efforts to Secure Taiwan

一六八三年，台灣成為清朝版圖，但是在官員眼中仍是容易出亂子的地方。

In 1683, Taiwan became a part of the Cing Empire, but most government officials still thought of Taiwan as fraught with the risk of an uprising.

中國
China

台灣
Taiwan

納入版圖後，清朝政府首先在台灣進行人口編查，並且規定在台灣沒有妻室產業的人要遷回內地。

After making Taiwan a part of their empire, the Cing Government conducted a census and ordered men who did not have families or their own farms to return to the mainland.

即使有妻室、產業，台灣的府縣也必須將戶口資料知會內地原籍的府縣嗎？

If a man had his own farm and family, did he still have to register his official family documents with the mainland province he came from?

沒錯！而且若有人犯罪，一律押回中國內地，永遠不許渡台。

That's right. And anyone found to have a criminal record was sent back to the mainland and never allowed back to Taiwan.

清朝政府治台政策的基本精神是為了防止有人在台灣聚眾生事。

The main theme of Cing Government policies was to prevent the people on Taiwan from uniting as a group.

在台灣南部的某地……
Somewhere in Southern Taiwan

鄭克塽投降，台灣換人管，新官府規定了一堆有的沒的，你聽說了嗎？

Jheng Keshuang has surrendered. Taiwan has a new ruler. They're making us follow a whole bunch of new rules. Have you heard?

當然聽說了！現在官員正在清查戶口，沒有妻室產業的人，要被趕回去。

Of course. The government is now checking everyone's official family documents. Men without families or farms will be sent back.

若任由百姓前去開墾，人口大量移入，日後治理恐怕更難周到了。

If we let many settlers go to Taiwan, the island will be difficult to govern.

大家有何應對之道？

How can we deal with this situation?

臣以為……

In my humble opinion …

你有何見解？

Speak up!

台灣位置地處邊疆，管理實屬不易，宜頒布法令，限制百姓渡台。

Taiwan is far away and difficult to control. I think we should restrict the number of people migrating to Taiwan.

吱吱
喳喳

咳！
咳！

怎麼個限制法？
What kind of restrictions?

據施提督的提議，沿海居民占地利之便，比較容易赴台開墾，而廣東一帶，久為海盜聚生之處，應嚴禁該地百姓渡台。

As Admiral Shih has pointed out, people living on the coast are close to Taiwan, and therefore have easy access. However, the province of Guangdong is full of pirates, so no one from there should be allowed to go.

嗯！有道理，繼續說下去。

Makes sense. Continue.

其他地方的人如果想要到台灣，必須先向官府申請，領到照單後才准渡台。

People from other provinces who want to go to Taiwan should be required to obtain a "Taiwan Entry Permit" from the authorities.

而且渡台者不准攜家帶眷，已經在台者，也不得招內地的親人前往。

Those going to Taiwan should not be permitted to bring their families over and those already in Taiwan should not be able to have relatives brought over.

真狠！

How heartless!

此舉可以避免渡台者在台生根，而且將家人留在內地如同人質，他們便不敢為非作歹。

This policy would not only prevent the residents from permanently settling, it would make their families virtual hostages. No one on the island would dare confront the government if his family were on the mainland.

這個辦法很好。
Excellent idea.

這下子一定會出很多問題。
This is going to bring trouble.

在福建閩南某地
Somewhere in southern Fujian

喂！心情可真好，從屋外都聽得見你在唱歌。
You're in a good mood. I heard you singing all the way down the road.

當然好囉！我丈夫說要接我到台灣去了。
I sure am. My husband in Taiwan said he wants me to join him.

51

不可能的，你胡說！
That's impossible. You must be kidding.

除了清查戶口並頒渡台禁令外，清朝政府有派兵到台灣嗎？
Other than conducting a census and imposing restrictions on migration, did the Cing Government also garrison Taiwan?

那是當然的，但是為了預防叛變，派駐兵力的方式也很特殊。
Of course. But to prevent mutiny, they made special rules about which soldiers could go and how long they could stay.

要把它設計成兵將不相習，派一個與這些兵員沒有關係的人當將領。

We'll put generals in command of soldiers who are unfamiliar with their commander and each other.

三年一任，以免長期留守台灣，脫離中央控制。

We'll only let them stay away from the mainland authority for a total of three years.

來台的官兵也不能攜眷，兵丁出缺也不准在台增補，這便是班兵制。

Soldiers were not allowed to bring their families to Taiwan. Also, the armies on Taiwan were not allowed to recruit soldiers from among the people already on the island.

果然設想周到。

They covered everything.

福建某處軍營
A Military Camp in Fujian Province

聽說朝廷要抽人到台灣去，你想不想去？
I heard the government is going to pick soldiers to go to Taiwan.

要看運氣，不是每一個人都能去。
It'll take some luck to be one of the chosen few.

希望老天爺保佑，讓我過去。
I hope a trip to Taiwan is in the stars for me.

唉！一任才三年，能做什麼呢？
You only get to stay for three years. That's too short.

你不懂啦！
You don't understand what a chance this is!

觀世音菩薩、如
來佛、太白星君
、齊天大聖……

I'll pray to the Taoist
gods and Buddhist
gods and …

你少烏鴉嘴。
Don't say such things.

一切都是命，現在才求
神拜佛，來不及了。
Our fates are predetermined.
It's too late to start praying to
the gods.

林大福！
Mr. Lin!

是我，我中了！
That's me. I was
picked!

由於兵員來自各個不同的營區，又無固定統將，加上三年輪調制，軍隊任期有一半時間花在旅途上。

Because the soldiers came from different camps and served under many different commanders, the process of collecting troops and sending them to and from Taiwan took about a year and a half — half of the soldier's term of duty!

老天爺真幫忙，真的讓我去台灣。

The gods really watched over me. I'm going to Taiwan!

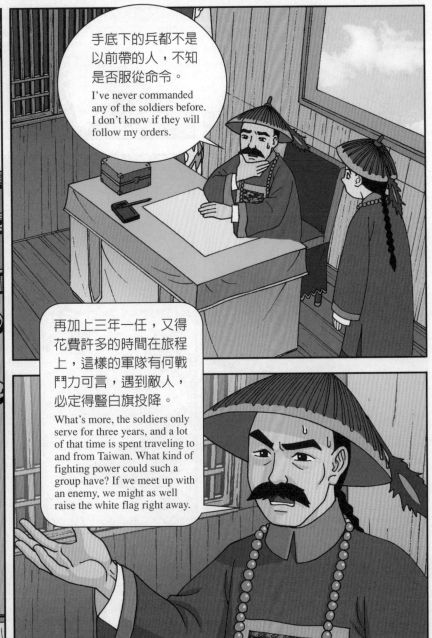

兩年後……
Two years later ...

換我吧，你該進去收拾行李了。
I'll take over. You should go inside and pack.

怎麼才剛到，就要走了？
I feel like we just got here.

沒辦法，三年一調，路程又這麼遠，不早點離開，趕不及回去報到。
Our term of duty is only three years long. If we don't leave early, we won't get back to the mainland on time.

老實說，你真的想走嗎？

Honestly speaking, do you really want to leave?

台灣這麼好，實在捨不得走啊！

Taiwan's great. I can't stand the thought of leaving.

不如我們留下吧！

Why don't we just stay!

留下？

Stay?

到了晚上⋯⋯

After dark ...

快點，你很重耶！

Hurry up! You weigh a ton!

好啦！小聲點，被人發現就走不了了。

Be quiet! If they catch us we'll never get out of here.

噓！安靜點。

Shhh! Keep quiet.

當時班兵軍紀敗壞，不僅私設賭場、當鋪，並且時有逃兵，所以每次遇到重大亂事，總得仰仗中國內地調來的專征部隊。

The Cing policy of stationing troops on Taiwan was a failure. Not only did the soldiers set up casinos and pawnshops, a good number of them even deserted. The troops were so unreliable that whenever serious problems arose among the settlers, the government had to call for assistance from the mainland army.

清朝政府為了防止民間私藏武器，限制生鐵和鐵器輸入台灣，人民也不能自由鑄造鐵器。

To prevent the residents of Taiwan from having their own weapons, the Cing Government prohibited the import of raw iron and iron implements. Settlers were not allowed to make iron implements either.

哇！壞了。
Oh no, my hoe broke!

你真是不小心，鋤頭很難買的。
How careless! Buying a new hoe is really difficult.

當時製造鍋具、農具的人必須向政府申請，由官府發照，稱為「鑄戶」，全台總共才二十七家。

A man who wanted to make pots and agricultural equipment for a living had to apply for a license. If his application were accepted, his family would become an official "blacksmith family". There were only 27 such families in Taiwan.

清朝政府認為台灣之亂起於內，不起於外。也就是說台灣如果安全上有問題，那是台灣內部產生的，不是因為外敵，所以台灣不准築城牆。

The Cing Government believed that trouble in Taiwan would come from a revolt by the islanders themselves, not from an attack by outsiders. In other words, Taiwan's threat was internal, not external. Therefore, castles were not allowed on Taiwan.

不過，如果內亂發生時，城牆便有可能被叛亂者占領，反而成為叛亂者的防禦利器。

However, if a rebellion occurred on the island and the rebels overtook the castle, it would become a powerful defensive weapon for them.

可是如果有外患的話，城牆可用來防禦，讓外患無法攻入得逞啊！

If there were an attack from the outside, castle walls would keep the attackers out.

叛亂王

台灣盛產竹子，種植成叢的刺竹做為防禦屏障，在當時很普遍。因此，官府所在地，例如竹塹（新竹）、諸羅（嘉義）都有「竹城」。

Bamboo has always been plentiful on Taiwan. During the Cing era, planting groves of bamboo trees to serve as a stockade was a common practice. Government headquarters, for instance those in Jhucian (today's Hsinchu) and Jhuluo (today's Chiayi), were surrounded by thick bamboo stockades.

就連民間也在村落或是家屋外圍種植刺竹做為屏障。

Villages and even single homes planted bamboo groves to serve as protective barriers.

清朝政府為防止台灣發生亂事，定了許多法令。

The Cing Government enacted many laws aimed at preventing rebellion on Taiwan.

渡台 NO！ No Immigration

在台徵兵 NO！ No Local Recruiting

私買鐵器 NO！ No Iron Implements

築城 NO！ No City Walls

但還是不放心，又下令來台者不准入山。

But the government was still worried, so they made a law prohibiting Chinese from entering the mountains.

禁止通行

這種政策一方面是在保護原住民，以免被華人欺負，另一方面則是怕華人進入山區，官府管不到，據險作亂。

On the one hand, the government wanted to protect the indigenous peoples from being abused by the Chinese; on the other, they wanted to prevent Chinese rebels from using the high, steep mountains as a natural fortress.

土牛就是以土堆積成壘，外形像躺著的牛，而「紅線」就是……

The ditches were called "ox backs" because the mounds on either side of them looked like the backs of oxen. The borders were called "red lines" because …

官府劃定界線，並在界線上挖築土牛溝，華人越過界線，會遭到重罰。

The government dug ditches to indicate the borders between Chinese and indigenous territory. Chinese caught crossing these borders were severely punished.

是官府在地圖上劃出一條界線，表示華人可以墾耕的界線。

… they were written in red ink on official maps to indicate the frontier to which Chinese were allowed to settle.

界外
Off Limits

界內
Chinese Territory

在界線附近也可能會有木柵、土圍、竹圍，藉此防範原住民出草。

To keep the indigenous peoples from entering Chinese territory and killing the settlers, the borders were sometimes marked off with wooden fences, earthen mounds, or bamboo groves.

所以台灣現在還有與此相關的地名，像是土城、木柵等等。

Even today, Taiwan has many places named after these barriers, such as Tucheng ("Earthen Castle") and Mujha ("Wooden Fence")etc.

木柵
wooden fence

土圍
earthen mounds

竹圍 bamboo groves

清朝政府為了防台而制定多項政策，進而用這些規定治理在台灣的人民。

Many of the laws and policies the Cing Government created to govern the people of Taiwan were designed to prevent rebellion.

小朋友如果仔細留意周遭，也許你也會發現因清朝時期的這些政策，而留下來的歷史遺跡喔！

Look around and you will find the remnants of Cing era policies, but you'll have to be a good history detective.

渡台禁令，禁什麼？

　　清朝政府統治台灣後，害怕台灣再度成為作亂者的基地，對於華人來台灣設了許多禁令，但這些「禁令」有些時候不能被徹底執行，甚至以後也陸續取消了。

　　這些「禁令」在禁什麼，你還記得嗎？就如同下圖所列。

　　哇！「禁」這麼多，清朝皇帝一想到台灣，大概就心神不寧。但是，清代從中國來台灣的人數還是年年不斷增加。

禁止攜眷。

限制人員來台。

禁止私製鐵器。

禁止入山開墾。

禁止築城牆。

清代士兵輪番戍守台灣，三年一調。

必須申請照單。

清朝政府對中國人民渡台的禁令時鬆時緊。

第3章
閩粵人的樂土

An Earthly Heaven for the Fujianese and Cantonese

滿清統一中國後，社會、經濟復甦，人口急速增加，在康熙末年（十八世紀初）已達到飽和點。人口壓力之大，東南沿海的閩、粵兩省尤其名列前茅。

After the Cing Government took over China, the country's economy recovered and many social problems were resolved. By the beginning of the 18th century, China was overpopulated. The coastal provinces of Fujian and Guangdong were particularly packed.

在福建某處
Somewhere in Fujian Province

唉喲！
Ouch!

對不起，
我不是故意的。
Sorry! I didn't do it on purpose.

都瘀青滲血了。
My leg's black and blue.

還好吧？
Are you OK?

好痛哦！喂！
下次小心點。
That hurt! Be careful next time.

田地就這麼一小塊，要耕種的人太多了，大家就互相讓一讓吧！
With so many people trying to work this little plot of land, accidents are inevitable.

日子不好過，就忍耐一下。
We're going through bad times. Be patient.

相對於中國內地的生活緊迫，在海的另一邊的台灣，卻是個謀生容易的地方。

While mainlanders were scraping to eke out a living, people on Taiwan were making a living with ease.

而且土壤肥沃，不需施肥，就可耕種。

The soil is so rich you can start farming right away—no need to fertilize.

高溫多雨的氣候，利於農作物生長。

The warm, wet climate is just right for farming.

由於農作物收成好，每年有大量的餘糧可運往對岸，台灣成為提供中國東南地方糧食的大穀倉。

Every year Taiwan harvested a bumper crop of fruit and rice. Taiwan's large surplus was shipped to the mainland and Taiwan became the granary for much of southeast China, supplying food staples.

這裡有許多水果，像是芒果、波羅蜜，還是中國內地所沒有的呢！

Look at all these different fruits. They don't have tropical fruits like mangoes on the mainland!

但是，由於生活容易，在台灣的人衣食較中國內地奢靡。

Because life on Taiwan was more comfortable than on the mainland, many of the people on the island became less frugal. Some became downright wasteful.

乾！不醉不歸。
Come on, drink up!

不好意思，酒灑到你的衣服上了。
Oh, sorry. I got rice wine all over you.

沒有關係，再買就是了。
No problem, I can just buy a new shirt.

台灣的富庶豐裕，更顯現在婦女身上。據說城市的婦女中午過後，不分貴賤都穿著綾羅綢緞，坐著牛車去看戲。

Taiwan's affluence was apparent in the attire of the women. Historical records state that in the afternoons the women of the town could be seen wearing fine clothing riding in ox carts on their way to plays and performances.

台灣生活富裕的傳聞，加上中國內地人口壓力大，讓許多人對台灣心生嚮往。

When stories of the good life on Taiwan reached the ears of the people on the overcrowded mainland, Taiwan suddenly became the dream destination of many mainlanders.

中國內地
In China

喂！你發什麼呆？
What are you daydreaming about?

沒什麼。
Nothing.

看你，鋤頭都掉了，還說沒什麼。
Then why did you drop your hoe?

各位辛苦了，休息一會兒。

Everyone's been working so hard. You deserve a break.

別發呆，吃飯吧！

Stop dreaming and have something to eat.

唉！又是地瓜飯。

Not sweet potato and rice again!

有東西吃就不錯了。

It's better than going hungry.

一、二、三……

1, 2, 3 ...

你在數什麼啊？

What are you counting?

這碗裡只有三十六粒米。

I only have 36 grains of rice in my bowl.

去台灣很難的，
要申請照單。

It's not easy. You have
to apply for a permit.

這裡的生活是人過的嗎？一塊地那麼
多人耕作，怎麼吃得飽？就連碗裡有
幾粒米，都數得出來。

We can't live a decent life here. There are lots of
people working every little plot of land. How can
we get enough to eat? We can even count the
grains of rice in our bowls!

我想去台灣。

I want to go to
Taiwan.

不管用什麼辦法，
我一定要去台灣。

I'm going to Taiwan,
no matter what.

一個月後，在台灣某處……

One month later, somewhere in Taiwan

又下雨了。

It's raining again.

下雨才好，現在正是田地需要雨水的時候。

This is great. Rain is just what the crops need at this time of year.

來到台灣種田實在輕鬆許多，雨水豐沛，土地肥沃，不必施肥，稻米自己就會長出來，米粒又大得像豆子一樣。

Farming is so much easier in Taiwan. Plenty of rain, and the land is so fertile you don't even have to lay compost. Just plant the seed and up come grains of rice as big as soybeans.

儘管清朝政府頒布渡台禁令，但是台灣優越的生活環境，加上大陸人口壓力的推力，占地利之便的東南沿海居民仍源源不斷的湧向台灣。

Although the Cing Government prohibited immigration to Taiwan, the attraction of Taiwan's excellent living environment combined with the pressures of life on the overcrowded mainland forced a continual flow of coastal residents to spill out from Guangdong and Fujian Provinces and onto Taiwan's shores.

清代華人遷台路線

　　清代華人陸續渡台，迄二十世紀前夕，人口達二、三百萬，多為閩粵兩省籍，其中隸泉州、漳州籍者約十分之七、八，隸嘉應州、潮州籍者約十分之二，其餘隸福建其他各府及外省籍者僅百分之一。遷台後，泉籍多居海口與沿海平原，漳籍多居西部內陸平原及宜蘭平原，客籍多居近山平原及台地、丘陵地。

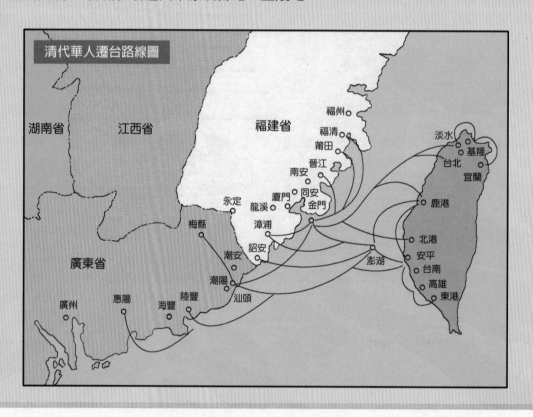

清代華人遷台路線圖

湖南省　江西省　福建省
福州
福清
莆田
晉江
南安
廈門　同安
永定　龍溪　金門
梅縣　漳浦
潮安　詔安
廣東省
潮陽
廣州　惠陽　海豐　陸豐　汕頭
淡水
基隆
台北
宜蘭
鹿港
北港
安平
澎湖　台南
高雄
東港

第 4 章
前仆後繼的偷渡

The Endless Tide:
Illegal Immigration to Taiwan

「唐山過台灣，心肝結歸丸。」一八七四年以前，清朝政府對渡台者有很多限制，但由於閩粵生活困難，台灣卻謀生容易，因此雖有禁令和台灣海峽之險，沿海居民還是不斷渡台。

"Since I left for Taiwan, my bitterness hardened like a stone." Prior to 1874, the Cing Government strictly limited immigration to Taiwan. However, poverty in the coastal areas of Fujian and Guangdong caused a continual flow of people to risk the dangers of the Taiwan Straits and confrontations with the law to get to a place where living was easier — Taiwan.

渡台照單申請處
Taiwan Entry Permit lineup

這次我花了大筆的銀兩，那位官員終於肯給我照單了。
I paid a lot of silver before I got the official to give me a permit.

妳真的很想去台灣？
You really want to go to Taiwan?

孩子的爹在那裡，我當然想和他團聚。
I want to be with my husband. I want my child to be with his father.

你是說走後門、送紅包給官員？可是我哪來這麼多錢。
I don't have enough money to bribe an official.

其實去台灣有很多種方法。
Actually, there are a lot of ways to get to Taiwan.

為了渡台，許多人冒險偷渡。有人冒充合法出海船隻的水手，有人藏在商船中偷偷出境，也有人直接買通官員私放。

Mainlanders used a variety of illegal means to immigrate to Taiwan. Some pretended to be deck hands, some stowed away in the cargo bins of merchant vessels, and some simply bribed the immigration officials.

當時有一種人稱為「船頭」或「客頭」，專門私載人出海。

Immigrant smugglers made a living transporting boatloads of illegal immigrants into Taiwan.

像我就是啦！

I smuggle people!

為了付錢給船頭，縮衣節食，典當各種東西，只為一圓渡台夢。

To pay off the immigrant smugglers, people saved every last coin and pawned every last possession—all for a chance of making the dream of going to Taiwan come true.

剩下這一些米，得省著吃才行。

This last bowl of rice grain will have to last us until we take off for Taiwan.

官府為防止人民偷渡，制定許多法令，嚴懲客頭、偷渡者及縱容包庇的官員，但是還是阻擋不了人民偷渡。

To prevent people from entering Taiwan unlawfully, the government created a law that strictly punished illegal immigrants, smugglers, and anyone found cooperating with or covering up for a smuggler.

這些衣服、棉被應該可以換到些許銀兩。

These clothes and this blanket ought to bring a couple pieces of silver.

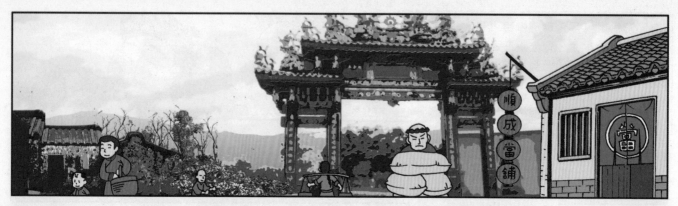

妳連棉被都拿來當！
You're even going to pawn your blanket?

沒辦法，得籌一筆錢去台灣。
I have to come up with money to go to Taiwan.

妳也知道棉被根本值不了多少錢，我只能給你這些。
You know a blanket's not worth much. I can only give you this.

不管多少都有幫助，謝謝你！
Anything will help. Thanks so much.

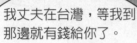

我丈夫在台灣，等我到
那邊就有錢給你了。
My husband's on Taiwan.
When we get there, he'll give
you money.

咚！

請你可憐可憐
孩子，載我們
過去吧！
Please have pity
on my child and
take us.

不行，不行。
No way.

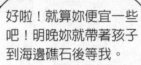

好啦！就算妳便宜一些
吧！明晚妳就帶著孩子
到海邊礁石後等我。
Well, I guess I could give you a
break on the price. It's a deal.
Bring your child to the big rock
on the beach tomorrow night.

謝謝！謝謝！
Thank you!
Thank you!

孩子，我們就快可
以和爹相聚了。
We're going to see
Daddy soon dear.

x

船頭將大船停在外海，夜間用小船到岸邊載人接到大海上，到了台灣外海時，再以小船接駁上岸，但船頭中有不少不肖之徒，許多透過他們偷渡的人不但損失財產，還賠上性命。

The captain of the smuggling ship would anchor in deep water outside the harbor. After nightfall he would send small boats to shore to pick up passengers. After reaching Taiwan, the same small boats would be used to bring passengers to their final destination. Passengers who met up with dishonest captains often lost their money, property, and even their lives.

是啊，就要到台灣享福了還哭，應該笑才是。

You'll soon be able to enjoy a happy life on Taiwan. Your child should be laughing, not crying.

哇！
Waah!

孩子，你別哭啊，會引來官兵的。

Don't cry dear, the guards will hear you.

小孩子的哭聲會引來官兵的，到時候大家會被捉，想想辦法別讓他哭，用被單悶住都好，不要讓他出聲吧！

If the guards hear him crying, they'll come and catch us all. Do something to keep him quiet. Stop his mouth with a blanket if you have to.

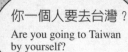

你一個人要去台灣？
Are you going to Taiwan by yourself?

去投靠朋友。妳是要去找妳的丈夫，對不對？
I'm going to meet up with a friend. You're going to join your husband, right?

嗯！官府規定在台者不能帶家人去，我只好帶著小孩偷渡。
The law says my child and I can't go. My only choice is to go over illegally.

我是受不了苦日子，單身一個人也申請不到照單，就冒險賭一賭了。
I can't stand the hardship anymore. Because I'm single, I can't get a permit, so I decided to risk this trip.

希望這一趟風平浪靜，別發生意外。
I hope we don't run into bad weather.

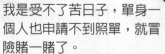

放心吧！
Don't worry.

看到了沒有，那才是要載你們過黑水溝的船隻。準備好，我們要換船了。

That is what will take you across the "Black Trench". Get ready to board ship.

上來以後，大家進船艙裡去。

After you get on board, go to the cabin below deck.

來，我幫妳。

Here; let me help you.

底下怎麼已經擠了這麼多人了？

What! This place is already packed with people.

妳以為只有妳想去台灣？給那麼少錢，還囉嗦個沒完，要麼就下去，不然就帶著小孩游過去。

Take it or leave it lady. For the price you paid, you shouldn't be complaining. Either shut up and get below with the others or jump off and try to swim across with your kid.

不肖的船頭將數百人擠入船艙內，並把艙蓋封釘，趁黑出海。

The captain would crowd hundreds of passengers into the belly of the ship, nail the entrance shut, and take off under the cover of the night.

借過！借過！
Let me by!

那是什麼聲音？
What's that noise?

好像有人在釘東西。
我上去看一看。
Sounds like someone's
nailing something.

唉喲！你踩
到我了。
Hey! You
stepped on my
foot.

船很擠，沒事不要
起來走動好不好？
The boat's crowded.
Don't move unless you
have to, OK?

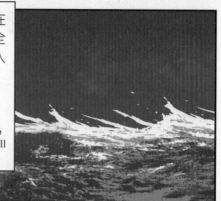

台灣與中國內地間的台灣海峽有處天險,在西南季風盛行、漲潮時,水流極快,水色全變,黝黑如墨,故有黑水溝之稱。船隻進入此區,稍有意外,便會船毀人亡。

At certain times of the year, one stretch of the Taiwan Straits is extremely dangerous. At high tide, the water becomes rough, fast and black as ink, thus in the Cing era it was called the "Black Trench". Once a sailing ship entered the Black Trench, a small mishap could very well mean the loss of the entire vessel.

把艙蓋封住的載人方式,若遇到大一點的風浪,船傾覆了,大家就完全沒有逃生的可能了。

Because the passenger cabin was nailed shut, if the ship capsized in a storm, none of the passengers would have even a chance of surviving.

可是這樣又怎麼確定到的地方就是台灣呢?

How would the passengers know for certain that the place they landed was Taiwan?

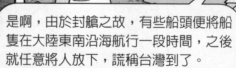

是啊,由於封艙之故,有些船頭便將船隻在大陸東南沿海航行一段時間,之後就任意將人放下,謊稱台灣到了。

Good question! Some dishonest captains took advantage of the fact that the passengers could not see outside. After sailing his ship along the coast for a while, the captain would drop the passengers somewhere on the mainland and tell them that they had landed in Taiwan.

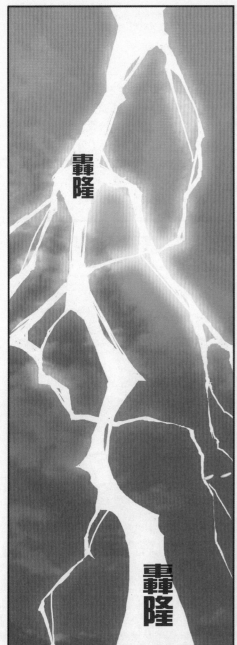

船晃得好厲害。
The boat is being tossed.

好像遇到暴風雨了。
Must be a rainstorm outside.

會不會有問題？
Will we be all right?

人人都說黑水溝很可怕，現在又加上暴風雨，只能求媽祖保佑了。
Everyone says the Black Trench is terrifying. Now we have bad weather on top of that. All we can do is pray.

嘔！

你還好吧？
Are you OK?

我頭好暈。
I'm dizzy.

船艙進水了。
We've sprung
a leak!

媽祖請保佑我們
平安到台灣。
Goddess Matzu,
please help us get to
Taiwan safely.

阿彌陀佛……

船到的時候，船頭為了怕被人發現，在外海沙洲上，就把人放下。

When the ship reached the coast of Taiwan, to avoid being spotted by government guards, often the smugglers would drop the passengers off on a sandbar in open water.

好像有動靜。

Something's happening on deck.

是不是台灣到了？

Have we arrived in Taiwan?

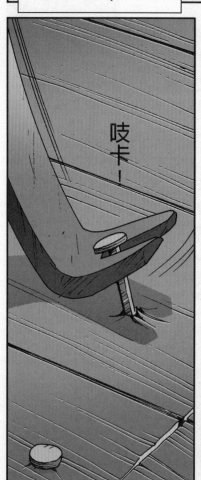

吱卡！

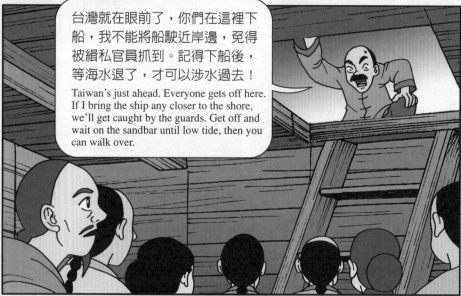

台灣就在眼前了，你們在這裡下船，我不能將船駛近岸邊，免得被緝私官員抓到。記得下船後，等海水退了，才可以涉水過去！

Taiwan's just ahead. Everyone gets off here. If I bring the ship any closer to the shore, we'll get caught by the guards. Get off and wait on the sandbar until low tide, then you can walk over.

啪答！

這土地好軟。
The sea floor is really soft.

唉呀！海邊土地都是這樣的，再往裡頭走就不會了。
That's what lagoons are like. The bottom gets firmer closer to shore.

你們自求多福，我走了。
Pray for good luck. See ya!

謝謝！再見！
Thank you. Bye!

他這麼壞，妳還跟他說謝謝。

Why do you want to thank such a wicked person?

......

人家總是把我們平安的送過黑水溝。

At least he brought us safely across the Black Trench.

走吧！再不走，天要亮了，到時會被官兵看見的。

Let's go while it's still dark. When daybreak comes the guards will be able to spot us.

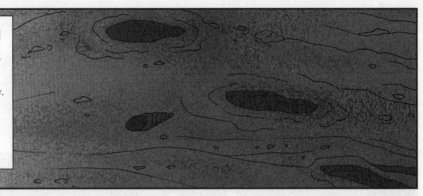

沙洲的土質鬆軟，離岸又很遠，走到較深處，會全身陷入泥淖，如果碰上漲潮，便會被海水淹死。

The floor of the sandbar was often soft and oozy. In deeper water, the sandbar could suck an immigrant's whole body down like quicksand. Also, the sandbar was often far away from the shore. If a high tide came up, the immigrants would drown in the deep water.

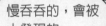

前面的人走得真快，一轉眼就不見了。

The people up ahead must be moving really fast. They just disappeared.

慢吞吞的，會被人發現的。

Let's get moving or we'll get caught.

那用跑的好了。

Let's run.

你看看周圍。
Look over there.

什麼！同船的人也掉入軟土裡。
Oh no! The others are being sucked down too!

今天滿月，海水會漲潮，我們會被淹死的，看來是到不了台灣了！
A full moon means high tide. We're going to drown. I guess we'll never see Taiwan.

我不甘心！
How can this be?

離台灣這麼近，卻沒辦法上岸，真是不甘心。

We got this close to Taiwan but weren't able to reach its shore. What a fate!

真是太美了！

Oh, how beautiful!

我們根本到不了台灣，妳居然還笑得出來。

How can you smile knowing we'll never reach Taiwan?

反正死定了，能看一眼，就心滿意足了。

We are going to die anyway. I got to see Taiwan. I'm satisfied.

孩子，看到了沒，爹在岸上對著我們笑呢！

Look dear, your father is on the shore smiling at us.

經過可能被騙，甚至葬身海底的重重考驗，僥倖到台灣的人，上陸地後還得躲避官兵的緝捕。

After having gone through many ordeals, those who reached Taiwan must face another difficulty – escaping the eyes of the government guards.

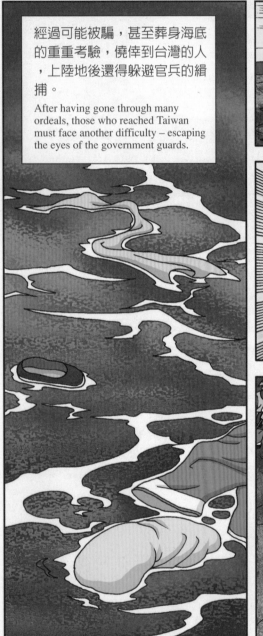

不要跑！你們逃不掉的。

Stop! You can't escape!

你們這是何苦呢？費盡千辛萬苦，到頭來還是被送回內地去。

You're all being sent back. All your pain and effort were for nothing.

為了過好日子，這樣是值得的。

For a better life, it's worth it.

是啊！難道你們駐守台灣，還會想回去嗎？

You know he's right. You don't want to go back to the mainland, do you?

真是可憐！

Poor people.

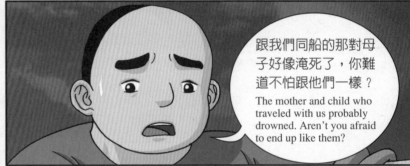

從中國內地渡台路途辛苦，有「六死三留一回頭」的說法。也有人以詩歌、民謠來記述這一段辛酸。康熙末年的藍鼎元有一首偷渡詩：

The journey to Taiwan was so risky that there was a saying: "Six in ten die, three stay and one sent back". There were many who recorded the bitter experiences of the immigrants in poems and songs. Lan Dingyuan wrote such a poem in early 1720s:

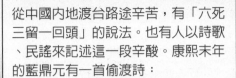

Who are those people there?
The illegal immigrants from the West.
Each dragging his chains,
Locked in his own sorrows.
You are driven by hunger.
But setting foot on shore,
You are caught by the guards.
What the fate of the foolish ones!
My tears make my sleeves wet.
Woo! Harsh is the law that bounds you,
Yet many keep coming and coming.

累累何為者？
西來偷渡人。
鋃鐺兼貫索，
一隊一辛酸。
嗟汝為饑驅，
登岸禍及身。
汝愚乃至斯，
我欲淚沾巾。
哀哉此屬禁，
犯者仍頻頻。

看來，藍鼎元應該是主張在台之人，都能帶家屬來台灣吧？

It seems that Lan Dingyuan was in favor of letting people bring their families to Taiwan.

是的。
You're right.

清朝地方官員有感於偷渡者源源不絕，防不勝防，捕不勝捕，先後向朝廷反映修改政策。

The government officials in charge of Taiwan saw the constant stream of illegal immigrants arriving at Taiwan and realized they could neither stop them all from coming nor catch them all when they arrived. Therefore, many officials made requests to the Imperial Court to change the policy.

在台者已有產業，不可能輕易回內地，勢必想盡方法，接內地的親人到台灣。如此一來助長偷渡風氣，成為不法之徒發財的保障。

Many of the people on Taiwan have already established their own farms or business and wouldn't want to leave all that to go back to the mainland. On the contrary, they are ready to do anything to bring their families over. This guarantees a big profit for the smugglers of illegal immigrants.

與其禁止攜眷渡台，還不如開放，那麼只要在台者有家室，便會專注在謀生上，而不會想為非作歹。

Instead of prohibiting the people of Taiwan from bringing families over, I think we should encourage them to do so. If the residents of Taiwan have families, they will concentrate on bettering their lives and won't think about opposing the government.

有些清朝地方官員甚至主張單身男子不准渡台，必須有家眷才能發給渡台照單。

Some Cing officials even advocated prohibiting unmarried men from going to Taiwan. Only men with families would have been able to get permission to go to Taiwan.

對於地方的呼籲，清朝政府曾數度准許內地人民攜眷入台，但是一般而言，還是不鼓勵民間到台灣開墾。

In response to the desire of so many mainlanders to travel to Taiwan, the Cing Government periodically relaxed restrictions and allowed families to immigrate. But, generally speaking, the Cing did not encourage mainlanders to go to Taiwan.

唐山到台灣之路，有禁令與海險的雙重阻礙，艱辛無比，但中國內地沿海居民還是前仆後繼突破海禁，越過海險，寫下一頁又一頁的渡台血淚史。

Though the trip from the mainland to Taiwan was arduous, the coastal people kept coming over, risking the perils of the sea and the penalties of the authorities. The stories of their treacherous, grueling journeys to Taiwan are written in blood and tears.

渡台悲歌

　　我們知道中國東南兩省，如閩（福建省簡稱）粵（廣東省簡稱）山多平原少，不斷增加的人口使得每人的可耕地更少。相較之下，地廣人稀的台灣就成為閩粵居民嚮往的樂土。

　　但是不是每一個來到台灣的人都能如願以償，在台灣很容易找到工作、耕地，甚至賺很多錢光榮回鄉呢？一則客家山歌「渡台悲歌」卻有不一樣的答案。

　　詩歌一開始說：「勸君切莫過台灣，台灣恰似鬼門關，千個人去無人轉，知生知死都是難。」許多人聽信客頭（帶路人）的話，以為在台灣賺錢很容易，於是散盡家財，千辛萬苦坐船來台。上了岸，想投靠親戚卻不受歡迎，只好自己找工作，受雇當一年的

長工。好不容易找到住的地方，卻是「自己無帳任蚊咬，自己無被任凍寒」。張羅棉被衣物就欠了老闆一筆錢，過年休假也被扣錢，這才發現老闆真是刻薄。在台灣吃得好嗎？「手扣飯碗氣沖天，一碗飯無百粒米……台灣番薯食一月，多過唐山食一年。」不禁嘆

道：想吃酒肉，下輩子再說吧！

　　至於工作的情形呢？每天早起工作到晚，「落霜落雪風颱雨，頭燒額遍無推懶。」就算生病也不敢請假，「唐山一年三度緊，台灣日日緊煎煎，睡到子時下四刻，米槌椿臼在礱間。」在家鄉一年只忙三回，在台灣卻是天天忙，早上一點就要起床椿米，接著要幫忙耕田，「天下耕田用腳踏，台灣耕田用手爬……天光跪到日落山，面目一身坭鬼樣，閻王看見笑連連。」

　　在台灣所見所聞常常令人生氣，覺得台灣是個「不敬斯文無貴賤」的地方。讀書人沒有讀書的樣子，而遇到喜慶這等大事，大家居然衣裝不整、打赤腳來參加，在宴席上相爭搶食就像餓鬼一樣。

　　沒有工作時，為了區區兩百錢也會冒著被馘首（割耳朵）的危險，像士兵一樣勇敢進入山區採黃藤，「放此台灣百物貴，唯有人頭不值錢，一日人工錢兩百，明知死路都敢行，抽藤做料當民壯，自己頭顱送入

山，遇著生番銃一響，登時死在樹林邊……不論男女並婦女，每年千萬進入山。」人命變得不值錢，也形容台灣已是謀生不易的地方。同時也可知道雖嚴禁入山，但當時已有許多華人積極前往山區了。

　　據推測，這首歌描述背景可能是十九世紀之後，渡台客族人的不幸遭遇。這時移民墾殖的黃金時代（可以因墾殖田園而獲大利，需要大量農工的時期）已經過去，因為不需要再多的農工墾地，來台找工作不再容易，就算受雇也是被老闆宰割。詩歌的最後說：「叮嚀叔侄併親戚，切莫信人過台灣，每有子弟愛來者，打死連棍丟外邊，一紙書音句句實，併無一句是虛言。」客族在台灣謀生的艱辛，溢於言表。

第5章
田園開發

Development of Land Cultivation

越過重重危險來到台灣的閩南人，用很快的速度在台灣開墾起來。

After making their way through innumerable trials and setbacks, the Hokkien (or Hoklo, people from southern Fujian) began cultivating the land at aremarkable pace.

一六八三年，台南以北只有一個諸羅縣，到了一七二二年，出現了第二個彰化縣。

In 1683, the only county north of Tainan was Jhuluo. In 1722, a second county, Changhua, was established.

從快速的往北設縣，可以看出人口急遽的增長與土地快速的開發。

The rapid establishment of northern counties is indicative of the rapid pace of population growth and land development.

在台開墾土地需要申請墾照，
並在無主荒地上才能開墾。

On Taiwan you had to obtain a permit
to cultivate the land and one could
only cultivate unclaimed land.

沒想到耕田這麼麻煩，
還得要申請。這麼多人
不知道要排到幾時？

I didn't know I needed a permit
to work the land. Look at the
size of that line.

像你這種沒關係
又沒錢的人很難
申請到的。

With no money or
connections, you'll
have a hard time
getting a land
cultivation permit.

當時有錢、有關係的人較容易拿到墾照，因此就有一些人專向官府申請開墾權利，然後再找人來耕種。

People with money and contacts could get land cultivation permits more easily. Such people would sometimes get a number of permits, then find farmers to work their land.

難道窮就註定命苦？

Must life be hard on the poor?

下一位！
Next!

這年頭有錢好辦事，我就是靠孔方兄跟官員混熟的，申請墾照對我來說是輕而易舉之事。

With the help of Mr. Money schmoozing the officials, getting land cultivation permits is a piece of cake for me.

照這麼說來，你有很多張墾照囉！

You must have a lot of permits.

我不是要你買下來，你只要每年按時交租金或農作物給我就行了。

You don't have to buy the land. Just pay me rent or a portion of your yield every year.

原來如此。那麼我就不必在這兒辛苦排隊申請墾照，也有田可以耕種。

I get it. I can have land to work without waiting forever in this line to get a permit.

是啊！像我不用親自下田耕種，只要將田放給佃農，就可以坐收田租了。

That's right. As for me, I don't even have to work the fields but sit back and collect rent.

我們就這麼說定了，大熱天的，別在這兒排隊了，喝茶去！

A deal! Let's get out of this long line and go drink some tea.

另外還有一種開發方式，便是聯合很多人出錢出力組成墾號（有如開墾公司）向官府申請墾照。

Another way of getting land was to contribute money to buy land development cultivation permits as a group (similar to modern day land development firms).

先合股開墾，不久之後就將財產和土地重做分配，各自管理經營了。

At first the group would cultivate the land together. Soon afterward, they would divide the land up and each person would cultivate his own portion.

集團性的開墾，有的以同族，有的以同鄉為結合，所以有些台灣地名還保留著同族開墾或同鄉開墾的痕跡，例如蘇厝莊、同安寮等。

Such land cultivation groups were generally founded based on clan or native village ties. Even today in Taiwan you can see traces of these groups in place names like Tung An Village (developed by people from Tung An, Fujian) and Sucuo Village (developed by Su clans).

五千，我出五千。
I can chip in 5,000.

那我也五千好了。
I can also give 5,000.

我三千啦！
I'll pitch in 3,000.

兩千可以嗎？
Is 2,000 OK?

行，大家這樣湊一湊，申請開墾應該沒問題了。

Getting a permit should be no problem then.

啪！

啪！

恭喜！
Congratulations!

恭喜！
Congratulations!

這全靠幾個同鄉的幫忙，才拿到墾照。
Only with the efforts of our fellow townsmen could we get the permits.

團結力量大，一個人申請墾照實在太累了。
Teamwork is effective.
A one-man effort is exhausting.

幾個月後……
Several months later ...

他們在那裡。
They're over there.

喂！我們在這兒！
Hey! Here we are.

你們終於來了，我們幾個守著這塊地，都快累死了。
Thank goodness you finally made it. We're exhausted working this land.

這裡跟家鄉差好多。
This place is a lot different than our hometown.

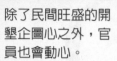

除了民間旺盛的開墾企圖心之外，官員也會動心。

The immigrants from the mainland were not the only ones aggressively cultivating the land. The government officials were ambitious too.

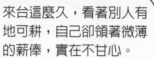

來台這麼久，看著別人有地可耕，自己卻領著微薄的薪俸，實在不甘心。

Ever since I came to Taiwan, I've watched the settlers get big fat pieces of land while I collect my measly salary.

就是啊！那點錢只夠吃飯配鹽。

It's unfair. Our salaries are barely enough to live on.

台灣這麼富裕，當官的俸卻少得可憐。

Taiwan is full of natural riches and we officials are poor as can be.

來，為我倆悲慘的命運乾一杯。
Let's drink to our bad luck.

說真的，你有沒有想過……
Hey, have you ever thought of …

你是說開墾？
You mean getting our own land?

是啊！
Exactly!

當時在台灣開墾的官員，不乏其人。
Many government officials cultivated land.

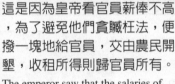

這是因為皇帝看官員薪俸不高，為了避免他們貪贓枉法，便撥一塊地給官員，交由農民開墾，收租所得則歸官員所有。
The emperor saw that the salaries of government officials were low. In an effort to prevent officials from taking bribes to supplement their income, the emperor gave them land which they could rent out to tenant farmers.

官田鄉
Guantien

台南縣
Tainan County

鄭氏時代有不少官有田園，在清朝政府接收之後，仍然交由官府管理，這類墾地被稱為「文武官田」。
Much of the land Cing authorities seized from the Jheng clan was still in government hands and, as such, was known as "official fields."

現在台南縣官田鄉就是非常有名的例子。施琅後代的「施侯租」也是官員收取地租的例子。
Guantien (literally means "official's field") Township in Tainan County is an example. The Shih clan, descended from Admiral Shih Lang, also enjoyed the right to rent out land.

施琅因征台之功，被封靖海侯，其後世子孫也可以襲封，受清朝政府特別恩寵。

The Cing Emperor rewarded Shih Lang for his successful takeover of Taiwan by giving him an honorary title: the Duke of Jinghai. Shih's descendents also received special treatment from the Cing Government.

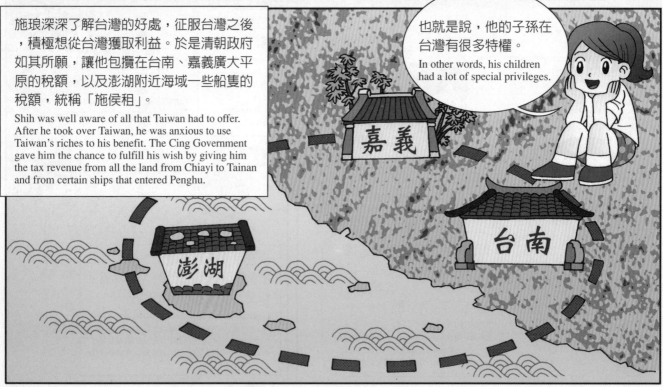

施琅深深了解台灣的好處，征服台灣之後，積極想從台灣獲取利益。於是清朝政府如其所願，讓他包攬在台南、嘉義廣大平原的稅額，以及澎湖附近海域一些船隻的稅額，統稱「施侯租」。

Shih was well aware of all that Taiwan had to offer. After he took over Taiwan, he was anxious to use Taiwan's riches to his benefit. The Cing Government gave him the chance to fulfill his wish by giving him the tax revenue from all the land from Chiayi to Tainan and from certain ships that entered Penghu.

也就是說，他的子孫在台灣有很多特權。

In other words, his children had a lot of special privileges.

嘉義

台南

澎湖

你們在看什麼？
What are you looking at?

朝廷給施家一大片台灣的土地，需要人去耕種。
The government gave the Shih family a large tract of land in Taiwan, so the shih's need extra farmhands.

在中國內地
In China

施家在台灣擁有龐大的產業，同時也嘉惠他的宗族和閩南同鄉。施家算是清初閩南地方最顯赫的家族。

The Shih family acquired large holdings in Taiwan and became patrons of their Southern Fujian clan and hometown. In the early Cing era, the Shih clan was the most prestigious family in southern Fujian.

那麼我們就是去台灣當施家的佃農囉？
So we're going to Taiwan to work as farmers for the Shih family?

是的。
Right.

康熙末年，在台灣中部開鑿水圳（又稱八堡圳），富甲一方的施世榜便是其宗族。

In 1720s the Shih family built a canal in central Taiwan (also known as Babao Canal) under the well-known Shih Shihbang, making them even more rich and powerful through collection of irrigation fees.

龐大的地租為施家累積財富與權勢。除了施琅之外，在台中的張國和藍廷珍也是官員開發的例子。不過，這和「文武官田」的開發不一樣，這是來台的官員看中台灣農墾的利益，私自招人開墾的。

Powerful landowning families like the Shih clan became more and more rich and influential.
In Taichung, officials Jhang Guo and Lan Tingjhen followed the example of the Shihs and cultivated land extensively. However, these men were not given land by the government; they acquired it on their own as an investment.

張國是總兵，藍廷珍是平定朱一貴之亂的提督。

Jhang Guo was a high-ranking military commander and Lan Tingjhen was the admiral who quelled the uprising of Jhu Yiguei.

張國
Jhang Guo

藍廷珍
Lan Tingjhen

張國仗著身為官員的權勢開發了一片土地，再設法讓官府購買下來，之後藍廷珍又轉攬開墾，這個地方稱為藍興莊，位於今日的台中市。

Jhang Guo used his status as a government official to first cultivate a large stretch of land, then arranged for the government to buy the land. The same land, what is now Lansing Village in Taichung, was then turned over to Lan Tingjhen for cultivation.

施琅家族和藍廷珍等官員，開墾的範圍都很大。

Government officials, such as the Shih family and Lan Tingjhen, cultivated vast areas of land.

與個人申請墾照相較，官員在開墾上真的占有很大優勢。

When it came to land development, government officials had a big advantage over ordinary citizens.

渡過黑水溝，來到台灣的華人，不分民間、官方都大力開發這片土地，實現他們在中國內地無法達成的夢想。

After crossing the Black Trench, government officials and commoners alike aggressively cultivated the land and made true many dreams that they could not have realized on the mainland.

番社采風圖的平埔族

　　現在我們要了解清代原住民的族群與生活，必須藉由當時人所留下的文字紀錄。例如一六九七年（康熙三十六年）郁永河的《裨海紀遊》；康熙末年巡台御史黃叔璥〈番俗六考〉、〈番俗雜記〉；地方志也都有對原住民風俗的描寫。

　　其中用「圖畫」記錄原住民生活情形的《番社采風圖》相當特別。乾隆年間，巡台御史六十七（一位滿人官吏，「六十七」是他的名字）特別請人繪製，要呈給清朝皇帝了解台灣原住民的情況。《番社采風圖》共有十二幅圖，畫出了原住民渡溪、耕種、收穫、獵捕、織布、住屋的情形。

其中右邊的這幅「捕鹿」圖，說明了當時北部淡防廳的大甲、後壠、中港、竹塹、霄裡等社的平埔族人，在秋末至初冬這段時期，聚集眾人出去捕鹿，稱作「出草」。我們可以看見原住民的打獵方式是一隊人一起出獵，讓狗跑在前面追趕獵物，再以箭矢射之。

這些圖畫都是當時歸附政府之「熟番」社內所見的情形。這些畫使我們對原住民有更活潑生動的了解。

清人繪製台灣原住民打獵情景。
（資料提供：國立中央圖書館台灣分館）

第 **6** 章
原住民的悲歌

The Sad Song of
the Indigenous people

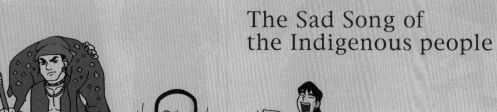

清朝政府將台灣納入版圖後，定了許多法令規範華人，當然政府也不忘規範原住民。清朝政府把原住民分為二類，接受教化並繳稅、服役的稱熟番，不服從以上規定的就稱為生番。

After making Taiwan part of its empire, the Cing Government created many new laws which Chinese and indigenous peoples alike were forced to obey. The Cing divided the tribes into two types: the "cooked" tribes, who paid taxes and performed services for the government, and the "raw" tribes, who refused.

看清楚了，我再教一遍，衣服是這樣穿的。

Watch closely. I'll demonstrate again.This is how you put on Chinese clothing.

華人認為生番是野蠻的，熟番較文明，而且熟番既然「慕義向化」，中國皇帝便有教化他們的義務。

The Chinese believed that the "cooked" tribes were closer to being civilized than the "raw" tribes, who were mere barbarians. Moreover, since the "cooked" tribes, as their name suggests, were ready and willing to improve, the Cing Government felt a responsibility to educate them.

哈！哈！
Ha, ha!

官府認為讓原住民薙頭、穿漢服，是變成所謂「文明人」的第一步。

The Cing officials on Taiwan believed that making the indigenous people shave their heads and wear Chinese clothing were the first steps toward civilizing them.

華人認為原住民「只知有母而不知有父」，便將中國的「父系」倫理觀念加諸他們身上，「賜」給原住民漢姓。

The Chinese were concerned that the indigenous people "only know their mothers but not fathers". They forced the indigenous people to adopt the idea of "patriarchial lineage" and "granted" them Chinese names.

聖上為獎勵你們慕義向化，特別賜姓給你們。

To reward you for your efforts to better yourselves, the emperor is granting you Chinese names.

這下我們全都得改名字了？

Now we have to change our names?

這樣吧，就賜給你們「潘」姓，有水有田，又有稻禾，很適合你們。

We'll give you the name "Pan". The Chinese character for Pan is perfect for you because it contains the symbols for water, rice plant, and rice field.

臣服王朝更具體的表現，即是繳稅、服役。

The "cooked" tribes showed their allegiance to the Cing by paying taxes and performing labor.

清朝政府在原住民社會實施包稅制，就是由包稅的人包攬原住民部落的稅，並負責去部落中徵稅。

The Cing Government assigned a tax collector to collect the tribes' taxes and hand them over to the government.

我就是社商。

I'm the Tax Collector.

這種包稅的人叫「社商」，他還可以在部落中進行買賣交易。

The Tax Collector was also allowed to conduct trade with the tribe.

今天該交稅了！

Your taxes are due today.

請再寬限一、二天吧！

Please give me just another day or two.

看在你上次賣鹿皮給我的份上，就再給你一天的時間。

Well, since you sold me deerskin last time, I'll give you an extra day to pay your taxes.

小老弟，真是體恤人，那就交給你辦。

You're a real team player. From now on, I'll let you do it.

沒問題，包在我身上。

No problem. You can count on me.

社商在取得包稅權後，通常不會親自收稅，而是委託給通事。

Instead of personally collecting taxes, the Tax Collector usually worked through the interpreter.

清朝政府在原住民各社都設有通事，負責傳達政令，多由華人擔任，後來演變成官方管理原住民的執行者，時常欺壓他們。

The interpreters, who were almost always Chinese, were sometimes appointed by the Cing Government to relate government orders to the indigenous people. Later, the interpreters often became the oppressors of the indigenous peoples.

原住民告官必須得靠通事翻譯，通事常從中作梗，所以原住民多忍住不告，有冤難伸。

Indigenous peoples who wanted to go to court had to rely on the interpreter. Predictably, the interpreter would often twist or change the meaning of an indigenous person's testimony, so the indigenous people learned to hold their tongues and swallow their anger.

你真是勤奮，一天獵了三隻鹿，晚上有好料可吃了。

You're a hard worker! Three deer in one day. We'll eat well tonight!

把口水吞回去吧，這不是給大家吃的。

Stop drooling! These deer are not for everyone.

你實在太小氣了，不分給大家吃。

Don't be stingy. Why won't you share?

我今天受了一堆氣，還會「小」氣！
Something happened that made me really angry.

到底怎麼一回事？
What on earth happened?

還不是通事，我已經繳稅金了，他硬是找藉口要我多給錢。我沒錢，他就要我獵三隻鹿送給他。
It's the interpreter again. I gave him the tax money I owed, but he came up with some excuse to ask for more. I had no money, so I had to hunt three deer for him.

嘻！
Ha!

嘻！
Ha!

噓！
Sihh!

唉呀！
Oh no!

小手都被溪水凍紅腫了。
Your little hand has turned red from the cold water.

呀！

你這麼心疼我的手，那你幫我洗吧！
If you're so concerned about my hands, why don't you do the washing?

我就知道你是不會拒人於千里之外。
I knew you wouldn't reject me.

啊！

啪咚！

強納原住民女子為妻妾，也是通事欺壓原住民的常有惡行。

The interpreters often forced indigenous women to become their concubines.

太可惡了！

That's terrible!

哈啾！

Aachoo!

主人，您保重。

Take care of yourself, Sir.

小小番女竟敢耍我，看我如何治你！

What nerve! I'll fix that savage girl.

通知她的父親，明天就把女兒給我送來。

Contact her parents. Tell them to send her to me tomorrow.

以後要聽話，不可像昨天那樣不乖。

In the future you'll have to be obedient. You can't behave like you did yesterday.

呸！

可惡！
You!

台灣納入清朝版圖後，原住民硬被套上與他們格格不入的生活方式，飽受欺壓。

After the Cing Government brought Taiwan into its empire, the Chinese settlers took advantage of every opportunity to abuse and oppress the indigenous peoples, who were forced to accept a lifestyle completely incompatible with their culture.

熟番歌

清朝政府將台灣的原住民分為兩種，一種是歸附政府，受政府管轄的「熟番」；另一種是居住在政府管轄區域之外（又稱「界外」）的「生番」。

「熟番」雖然不一定要納稅，但卻必須服勞役，政府有心想要保護這些「熟番」，但華人移民卻以各種手法騙取他們的土地、財產。至於「生番」因為生息於政府勢力所不及之地，政府也禁止華人移民越界偷墾，所以較不受侵擾。

一般來說，華人認為「熟番」愚直可欺，而認為「生番」兇猛，令人生畏。清朝地方官曾有「熟番歌」與「生番歌」來說明這種華人與原住民的關係，以及原住民的處境。以下是「熟番歌」的內容：

「人畏生番猛如虎，人欺熟番賤如土；強者畏之弱者欺，無乃人心太不古！熟番歸化勤躬耕，山田一甲唐人爭，唐人爭去餓且死，翻悔不如從前生。竊聞城中有父母，走向堂前崩厥首，啁啾鳥

語無人通，言不分明畫以手。訴未終，官若聾，仰視堂上有怒容。堂上怒呼將丈具，丈畢垂頭聽官諭：『嗟爾番！汝何言？爾與唐人吾子孫，讓耕讓畔胡弗遵？』吁嗟乎！生番殺人漢人誘，熟番翻被唐人醜，為民父（母）者慮其後。」

　　「唐人」指的就是華人移民。作者感嘆世風日下，華人見「熟番」可欺，常常奪取他們的土地，使他們失去生活的憑藉而痛苦萬分。作者描述一位「熟番」的土地被華人奪走，聽說縣城中有號稱「人民父母」的縣官（身負行政與司法責任的地方縣令），於是到縣衙門叩頭想請縣官作主。不料，原住民說的話這位縣官根本聽不懂，縣官越聽越生氣，不等他說完就將他打了一頓，並命令他把田讓一些給「一樣是同胞」的華人耕種。

　　「熟番歌」表現了清代前期華人對原住民的態度，及原住民土地被華人侵占的情形。另一個問題是「熟番」歸入政府管轄，官員對語言文化不同的族群沒有足夠的了解，更別說做出符合公平正義的判決。作者希望日後當父母官的要有所警惕，這其實不也是給現在的我們一個很好的提醒嗎？

《認識台灣歷史》第四、五、六冊共用此份年表

年代		台灣大事記
一六八四年	清聖祖康熙二十三年	◎清帝國將台灣納入版圖，設台灣府，隸屬福建省。建台灣府學及台灣、鳳山縣學。
一六八六年	康熙二十五年	◎客家人至下淡水平原（今日屏東）開墾。
一六九四年	康熙三十三年	◎知府高拱乾著《台灣府志》。
一六九七年	康熙三十六年	◎郁永河至北部採硫磺，一六九八年寫成《裨海紀遊》。
一六九九年	康熙三十八年	◎吞霄社原住民反抗通事暴虐；淡水、北投社反抗。
一七○九年	康熙四十八年	◎陳賴章拓墾大佳臘（今台北市西園）。
一七一一年	康熙五十年	◎清朝政府規定：凡是從內地（大陸）來台灣的人，必須在原籍地開具證明，並在期限內回去。
一七一四年	康熙五十三年	◎清朝政府規定：人民到大甲溪以北之處，必須得到官府允許；淡水地區被認為是不文明的「化外之地」。
一七一六年	康熙五十五年	◎岸裡社（今台中縣神岡鄉）原住民開墾貓霧揀。
一七一九年	康熙五十八年	◎施世榜開拓東螺堡、八堡圳。

年代		台灣大事記
一七二〇年	康熙五十九年	◎泉州人施長齡、吳洛，客家人張振萬等拓墾台北平原。
一七二一年	康熙六十年	◎朱一貴、杜君英反清，失敗被斬。 ◎阿里山、水沙連各社反抗通事（至一七二二年）。
一七二二年	康熙六十一年	◎南路閩粵械鬥，一七二三年又起。
一七二三年	清世宗雍正元年	◎清朝政府設置彰化縣，及淡水、澎湖廳。 ◎藍鼎元著《平台紀略》。
一七二四年	雍正二年	◎淡水拳山莊居民開拓霧里薛圳（景美、新店一帶）。
一七二七年	雍正五年	◎清朝政府不准攜眷過台。 ◎黃叔璥著＜赤崁筆談＞、＜番俗六考＞。
一七三〇年	雍正八年	◎台灣人無妻室者逐回原籍。
一七三二年	雍正十年	◎清朝政府准許人民攜眷來台。 ◎林武力聯沙轆、吞霄社圍彰化。
一七三四年	雍正十二年	◎嚴防人民渡台。
一七三八年	清高宗乾隆三年	◎建艋舺龍山寺。
一七三九年	乾隆四年	◎禁止華人進入「番地」。
一七四四年	乾隆九年	◎噍吧哖四社平埔族遷至荖濃溪與楠梓仙溪。
一七四五年	乾隆十年	◎泉州人沈用至錫口（今台北松山）拓墾，閩南人由鳳山到桃澗堡開墾。
一七四七年	乾隆十二年	◎客家人至貓裡（即苗栗）。

年代		台灣大事記
一七五五年	乾隆二十年	◎淡水擺接堡墾戶林成祖開闢大安圳（從中和到板橋至土城）。
一七五九年	乾隆二十四年	◎規定華人買番地，必須納「番租」。
一七六八年	乾隆三十三年	◎黃教攻擊岡山營房，焚大目降（今台南縣新化）汛房，攻斗六門。
一七八一年	乾隆四十六年	◎閩南人與平埔族秀朗社（今台北縣永和一帶）訂約開墾深坑埔。
一七八二年	乾隆四十七年	◎彰化因賭博爭執，引起大規模漳泉械鬥，水師為鎮壓亂事殺了兩百多人。
一七八六年	乾隆五十一年	◎鹿港龍山寺落成。
一七八七年	乾隆五十二年	◎林爽文之亂。 ◎禁止人民攜眷來台。
一七八八年	乾隆五十三年	◎實施屯番制。
一七九五年	乾隆六十年	◎吳沙占墾頭圍（宜蘭頭城）。 ◎陳周全反清。
一七九六年	清仁宗嘉慶三年	◎王士俊在竹塹開設私塾，鄭用錫等人入學就讀。
一七九七年	嘉慶四年	◎蛤仔蘭（宜蘭）因爭奪墾地引起泉籍、粵籍分類械鬥。
一八○四年	嘉慶九年	◎彰化平埔族在潘賢文率領之下，遷徙至蛤仔蘭。
一八○五年	嘉慶十年	◎海盜蔡牽攻擊淡水與鹿耳門等地，並劫走商船。
一八○九年	嘉慶十四年	◎淡水漳籍、泉籍之間的糾紛事件，引發分類械鬥並蔓延至彰化、嘉義。 ◎大龍峒保安宮落成。

年代		台灣大事記
一八一四年	嘉慶十九年	◎隘首黃林旺、陳大用、郭百年侵入水裡、埔里，至一八一七年官府將華人佃戶逐出埔里社，立碑禁止進入。
一八一七年	嘉慶二十二年	◎淡水廳在竹塹設立儒學。
一八二三年	清宣宗道光三年	◎噶瑪蘭軍工匠林詠春反清，攻青潭、大坪林。
一八二五年	道光五年	◎東勢角、葫蘆墩平埔族七百人遷移至埔里社。
一八三一年	道光十一年	◎客家人姜秀鑾、閩南人周邦正與官府合資設「金廣福」墾號，開拓北埔（在今新竹縣）。
一八三八年	道光十八年	◎英國人至淡水以鴉片換樟腦。
一八四一年	道光二十一年	◎英國納爾不達號（Nerbudda）在基隆觸礁，四百多人被俘、被殺。
一八五三年	清文宗咸豐三年	◎淡水發生漳泉械鬥，同安人敗退至大稻埕。
一八五八年	咸豐八年	◎天津條約簽訂，台灣開港。

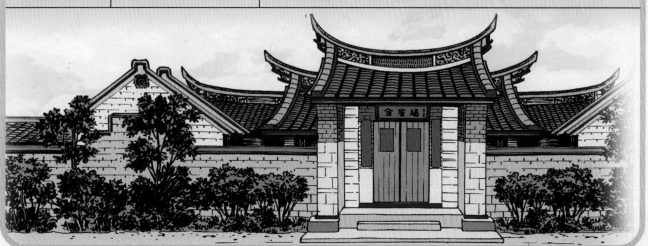

年代		台灣大事記
一八五九年	咸豐九年	◎北部多處（淡水港仔嘴、加蚋仔、枋橋、芝蘭莊、桃仔園）發生漳泉械鬥，延續至一八六〇年。
一八六〇年	咸豐十年	◎北京條約簽訂，開放淡水、安平港。
一八六二年	清穆宗同治元年	◎戴潮春反清。
一八六五年	同治四年	◎一八六四年戴潮春被捕，一八六五年嚴辦戰死，戴軍始衰。
一八六七年	同治六年	◎美籍船羅發號（Rover）事件。
一八七三年	同治十二年	◎牡丹社事件（至一八七四年結束）。
一八七四年	同治十三年	◎沈葆禎奉命辦理台灣等處海防。
一八七五年	清德宗光緒元年	◎設置台北府，管轄淡水、新竹、宜蘭三縣及基隆、卑南、埔里社三廳。

註：港仔嘴、加蚋仔、枋橋、芝蘭莊、桃仔園等地，即今日的江子翠、雙園、板橋、士林和桃園。

年代		台灣大事記
一八七六年	光緒二年	◎英人開八斗子煤礦。 ◎一八七六至一八七八年鎮壓東部原住民。
一八七七年	光緒三年	◎架設台南到旗後的電報線。
一八七八年	光緒四年	◎獎勵拓墾「番地」。
一八七九年	光緒五年	◎滬尾馬偕醫館成立。
一八八二年	光緒八年	◎馬偕創設牛津學堂，成為台灣北部第一間教授西學的學校。
一八八三年	光緒九年	◎中法越南戰爭。一八八四年起法軍封鎖北部台灣，並占領澎湖。
一八八五年	光緒十一年	◎台灣建省。
一八八六年	光緒十二年	◎設南北兩府清賦總局，在台北設置電報局、茶厘、稅厘、礦務總局。
一八八七年	光緒十三年	◎清朝政府籌辦台灣鐵路，並連接台灣與福州（福建）的海底電報線。
一八八八年	光緒十四年	◎設郵政總局；實施由小租戶直接納稅。

發現台灣，考考你！

看漫畫書好玩吧，你對台灣的歷史有更多的認
識了嗎？下面的題目可以讓你和父母、老師、
朋友們討論，分享彼此的想法。一起走進歷史，
發現台灣吧！

1 清朝政府反對台灣納入版圖，施琅為什麼獨排眾議，
極力主張收台灣入版圖呢？

2 清朝政府為防止台灣發生亂事，做了很多措施，
你覺得有用嗎？

3 動動腦，
土城、木柵這些地方與清朝政府的哪些政策有關呢？

4 清朝政府為什麼限制百姓渡台？
有哪些人不准去？

5 為什麼中國東南沿海居民會不顧危險橫渡來台呢？

6 你知道「黑水溝」指的是什麼嗎？

7 「六死三留一回頭」是形容渡台的艱辛，
你知道當時的人在渡台的路上會遭遇哪些危險嗎？

8 古有「唐山過台灣」，今有「大陸偷渡客」，
你覺得兩者有什麼不一樣呢？

9 蘇厝莊、同安寮等是因為什麼樣的開墾方式而有的地名呢？

10 清朝政府鼓勵原住民「慕義向化」，
但「慕義向化」表示在生活上要有什麼樣的改變呢？

製作群介紹

◎ 總策劃
吳密察
現職：台灣大學歷史系副教授
學歷：日本東京大學博士課程修了，專攻台灣史、
　　　日本近代史

◎ 漫畫繪製
朱鴻琦
現職：[德摩創意多媒體股份有限公司] 負責人
學歷：中國文化大學大眾傳播系畢業

◎ 漫畫繪製
葉銍桐
現職：專業漫畫家，曾任卡通動畫師
學歷：協和工商美工科畢業

◎ 劇本編寫
陳婉箐
現職：報社編輯，寫作多本漫畫劇本
學歷：台灣大學歷史系畢業

◎ 附錄資料撰寫
陳雅文
現職：編輯
學歷：台灣大學歷史系畢業

◎ 英文版策劃
文魯彬（Robin J. Winkler）
現職：台灣蠻野心足生態協會理事長、博仲法律事
　　　務所（本國與外國法事務律師事務所）合夥
　　　律師。1977年旅居台灣，於2003年放棄美
　　　國籍後，歸化為中華民國國籍。

◎ 英文審訂
翁佳音
現職：中央研究院台灣史研究所助研究員
學歷：台灣大學歷史研究所碩士，曾留學荷蘭萊頓
　　　大學（Leiden）攻讀歐洲擴張史；專攻十七
　　　、八世紀台灣史

◎ 英文審訂
賴慈芸
現職：台灣師範大學翻譯研究所助理教授
學歷：香港理工大學中文及雙語研究系博士

◎ 英文審訂
耿柏瑞（Brian A. Kennedy）
現職：博仲法律事務所（本國與外國法事務律師事
　　　務所）編譯員
學歷：美國馬里蘭大學新聞學及東亞學雙學位

◎ 英文翻譯
白啓賢（Matthew Clarke）
現職：美國密西西比州Nissan公司日語翻譯員
學歷：美國密西根大谷州立大學畢業

Editorial Staff

◎ Editor-in-Chief
Wu Mi-cha
Wu Mi-cha is an associate professor with National Taiwan University's Department of History.
He received an M.A. degree from the University of Tokyo's Graduate School of Arts and Sciences, specializing in Taiwan history and the history of modern Japan.

◎ Cartoon Illustrator
Chu Hung-chi
Chu Hung-chi is director of Demos Imagetech Co., Ltd. He holds a B.A. in mass media from Chinese Culture University.

◎ Cartoon Illustrator
Yeh Chi-tung
Yeh Chi-tung is a professional cartoonist and former cartoon animation specialist. He received an associates' degree in fine arts from Sieho College of Commerce.

◎ Cartoon Script
Chen Wan-ching
Chen Wan-ching is a Chinese-language newspaper editor. She is the author of several comic book scripts.

◎ Editorial Researcher
Grace Chen
Grace Chen works as a newspaper editor. She holds a B.A. degree in history from National Taiwan University.

◎ Chief English Editor
Robin J. Winkler
Robin J. Winkler is director of the Taiwan Wild at Heart Legal Defense Association and founding partner of Winkler Partners, Attorneys of Domestic and Foreign Legal Affairs. Having come to Taiwan in 1977, he gave up his U.S. citizenship to become a naturalized citizen of Taiwan in 2003.

◎ English Editor
Ang Kaim
Ang Kaim is a research fellow at Academia Sinica's Institute of Taiwan History. He received an M.A. degree in history from National Taiwan University.
He studied the History of European Expansion at Leiden University in the Netherlands, specializing in the history of Taiwan during the 17th and 18th centuries.

◎ English Editor
Sharon Lai
Sharon Lai is assistant professor at the Graduate Institute of Translation and Interpretation, National Taiwan Normal University. She received her Ph.D. in Chinese and bilingual studies from Hong Kong Polytechnic University.

◎ English Translator / Series Editor
Brian A. Kennedy
Brian A. Kennedy is a legal translator for Winkler Partners. He holds a combined B.A. degree in Journalism and East Asian Studies from the University of Maryland.

◎ English Translator
Matthew Clarke
Matthew Clarke is a Japanese translator for Nissan Automotive in Jackson, Mississippi. He holds a B.S. degree in political science from Grand Valley State University in Michigan.

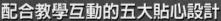

建議以下對象必讀
Recommended as a "must-read" for the following:

1 國小中高年級、中學生
Older primary and middle school students
認識台灣歷史、增進英文的最佳課外讀物

2 中小學教師
Primary and middle school teachers
教學上最佳輔助本土教材、英文教材

3 學校圖書館
School libraries
借閱率最高的必備好書

4 外國友人
Foreign friends
輕鬆認識台灣的第一本書

5 所有新台灣人
Every "New Taiwanese"
了解台灣歷史必讀入門書、人人都可以用
英文為外國人介紹台灣

了解台灣，從《認識台灣歷史》開始 A greater understanding of Taiwan starts with "A History of Taiwan in Comics"

1 遠古時代：南島語族的天地
Ancient Times: Austronesian Origins

2 荷蘭時代：冒險者的樂園
The Dutch Era: A Paradise for European Adventurers

3 鄭家時代：鄭氏集團的興衰
The Koxinga Period: The Rise and Fall of the Jheng Regime

4 清朝時代（上）：唐山過台灣
The Cing Dynasty (I): Leaving the Mainland for Taiwan

5 清朝時代（中）：羅漢腳的世界
The Cing Dynasty (II): The World of the "Wandering Bachelors"

6 清朝時代（下）：戰爭陰影下的建設
The Cing Dynasty (III): Construction Under the Shadow of War

7 日本時代（上）：日本資本家的天堂
The Japanese Era (I): The Backyard of Japan's Capitalists

8 日本時代（下）：覺醒的年代
The Japanese Era (II): The Age of Awakening

9 戰後（上）：強人天空下
The Post-World War II Era (I): In the Realm of the Strongmen

10 戰後（下）：改革與開放
The Post-World War II Era (II): Reform and Openness

○○○ 全套買省更多 ○○○

典藏版10冊＋電子書1片／全套3500元
普及版10冊／第1冊149元，第2-10冊，每冊250元／全套買省更多，歡迎來電洽詢最新優惠方案。

Save even more on a complete set: Hardcover 10-volume edition + CD-Rom: NT$3500
Paperback 10-volume edition: NT$2399; Individual volumes: Volume 1, NT$149; Volume 2 through 10, NT$250 per volume.
Call for details on the latest promotions.

訂購專線：886-2-27845369
Call to order: 886-2-27845369

劃撥帳號：17239354／新自然主義股份有限公司
Purchasing Information: http://www.thirdnature.com.tw

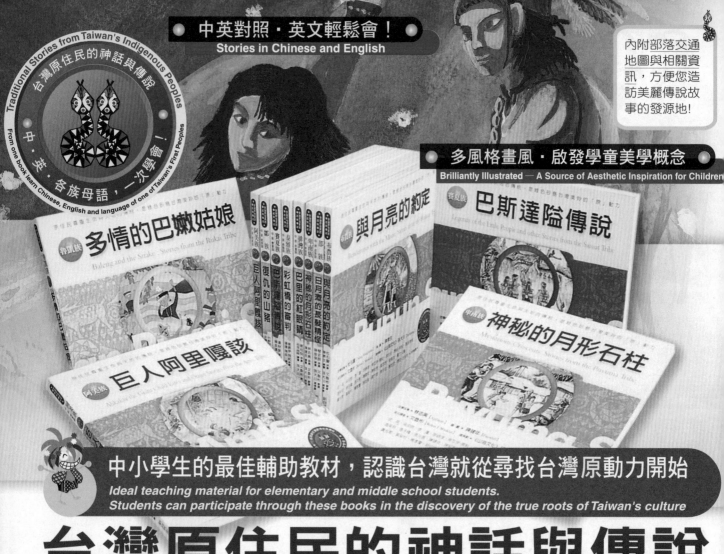

感謝專家學者肯定推薦

- 史 英 ・吳密察 ・李 潼・李錫津 ・帝瓦伊-撒耘・浦忠成
- 馬紹-阿紀・高金素梅・高榮欽・張子樟 ・張炎憲 ・陳建年
- 陳郁秀 ・曾志朗 ・曾憲政・動力火車・黃光男 ・黃榮村
- 楊孝濚 ・趙自強 ・蔣竹君・蔡中涵 ・謝世忠 ・懷劭-法努司

本書七大特色

1. 傳神生動的台灣原住民故事，搭配色彩豐富的圖畫，讓我們更親近及認識台灣。
2. 結合各族原住民作家採集傳說神話故事，題材多元豐富，並為口傳歷史留下文字見證。
3. 原住民藝術家提供精采插圖，生動呈現傳說故事圖像，令人身歷其境。
4. 每則故事都有中英文對照，並附原住民母語詞彙以及問候語，三種語言一次通。
5. 附「挑戰原住民Ｑ＆Ａ」、「部落百寶盒」、「ｅ網情報站」方便教師教學與學生複習。
6. 詳解故事精神與意義，萃取原住民生活經驗及與大自然和諧共生的哲理。
7. 古今對照神話故事發生地，附錄各族景點，是學校戶外教學及深度旅遊最佳參考資料。

誰最適合閱讀

1. 國小中高年級、國中生最佳課外讀物。
2. 父母家長最新鮮的說故事題材，適合親子共同閱讀。
3. 中小學教師從事原住民教育及原住民母語教學最佳輔助教材。
4. 國內外圖書館、原住民文化展覽館或博物館必備參考書。
5. 發揚及傳承原住民文化的最佳推廣普及工具書。
6. 國外友人，了解台灣原住民文化最佳入門中英對照書。
7. 提供喜愛台灣原住民文化的讀者賞析及珍藏使用。

全系列共10冊

◎ 卑南族：神秘的月形石柱
Mysterious Crescents: Stories from the Puyuma Tribe
故事採集：林志興・繪圖：陳建年

◎ 賽夏族：巴斯達隘傳說
Pas-taai:Legends of the Little People and other Stories from the Saisiat Tribe
故事採集：潘秋榮・繪圖：賴英澤

◎ 布農族：與月亮的約定
Rendezvous with the Moon: Stories from the Bunun Tribe
故事採集：杜石鑾・繪圖：陳景生

◎ 排灣族：巴里的紅眼睛
Pali's Red Eyes and Other Stories from the Paiwan Tribe
故事採集：亞榮隆・撒可努・繪圖：見維巴里

◎ 邵族：日月潭的長髮精怪
The Long Haired Spirit of Sun Moon Lake: Stories from the Thao Tribe
故事採集：簡史朗・繪圖：陳俊傑

◎ 達悟族：飛魚之神
The Flying Fish Spirit and Other Stories from the Tao Tribe of Orchid Island
故事採集：希南・巴娜妲燕・繪圖：席・傑勒吉藍

◎ 泰雅族：彩虹橋的審判
The Rainbow's Judgment: Stories of the Atayal Tribe
故事採集：里慕伊・阿紀・繪圖：瑠瑠・瑪邵

◎ 鄒族：復仇的山豬
Revenge of the Mountain Boar and Other Stories from the Cou Tribe
故事採集：巴穌亞・迪亞卡納 / 繪圖：阿伐伊・尤于伐那

◎ 阿美族：巨人阿里嘎該
Alikakay the Giant and Other Stories from the Amis Tribe
故事採集：馬耀・基朗 / 繪圖：林順道

◎ 魯凱族：多情的巴嫩姑娘
Baleng and the Snake: Stories from the Rukai Tribe
故事採集：奧威尼・卡露斯 / 繪圖：伊誕・巴瓦瓦隆

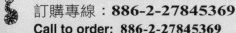
訂購專線：886-2-27845369
Call to order: 886-2-27845369

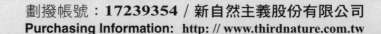
劃撥帳號：17239354 / 新自然主義股份有限公司
Purchasing Information: http:// www.thirdnature.com.tw

國家圖書館出版品預行編目資料

認識台灣歷史.4, 清朝時代(上)：唐山過台灣
= A History of Taiwan in Comics. 4,
The Cing Dynasty (I)：Leaving the
Mainland for Taiwan / 陳婉箐劇本編寫；
[德摩創意]朱鴻琦、葉銍桐漫畫繪製；白啟賢
（Matthew Clarke）英譯. --初版. --臺北市：
新自然主義. 2005〔民94〕
　　面：　公分
中英對照
ISBN 957-696-565-9（精裝）
ISBN 957-696-581-0（平裝）

1. 臺灣 - 歷史 - 漫畫與卡通

673.22　　　　　　　　　　　　　93016525

認識台灣歷史 ❹

原《漫畫台灣史》增訂

A HISTORY OF TAIWAN IN COMICS

清朝時代(上)：唐山過台灣
The Cing Dynasty (I): Leaving the Mainland for Taiwan

總策劃：吳密察
漫畫繪製：[德摩創意] 朱鴻琦、葉銍桐
劇本編寫：陳婉箐 / 資料編寫：陳雅文
英文版策劃：文魯彬（Robin J. Winkler）
英文審訂：翁佳音、賴慈芸、耿柏瑞（Brian A. Kennedy）
英文翻譯：白啟賢（Matthew Clarke）

初版：2005年1月
一版六刷：2008年6月
典藏版定價：新台幣350元
普及版定價：新台幣250元
郵撥帳號：17239354　新自然主義股份有限公司
地址：台北市建國南路二段9號10樓之2
電話：886-2-27845369
傳真：886-2-27845358
網址：www.thirdnature.com.tw
E-mail：moonsun@ms18.hinet.net

版權所有・翻印必究　Printed in Taiwan
本書如有缺頁、破損、倒裝，請寄回更換。
ISBN 957-696-565-9（精裝）
ISBN 957-696-581-0（平裝）

出版者：新自然主義股份有限公司
發行人：洪美華
總編輯：蔡幼華
專案統籌：黃信瑜
責任編輯：高美鈴
編譯協力：王興安、馮瓊儀、關山行（K. Mark Brown）
版型設計：唐亞陽工作室
美術設計：陳巧玲
編輯部：劉又甄、何靜茹、蔡喬如
市場部：張惠卿、劉秀芬、徐雪敏、黃麗珍
管理部：洪美月、巫毓麗、陳候光、鄭欽祐

製版：凱立國際資訊股份有限公司
印刷：久裕印刷事業股份有限公司

總經銷：農學股份有限公司
台北縣新店市寶橋路235巷6弄6號2樓
電話：886-2-29178022　傳真：886-2-29156275

Call to Order: 886-2-27845369
Website: www.thirdnature.com.tw

特別感謝「博仲法律事務所」（本國與外國法事務律師事務所）的協助。

一部最精采有趣、具學術基礎、完整又翔實的台灣史
適合9到99歲的大人小孩閱讀

知識漫畫版《認識台灣歷史》（全套10冊），

不但中英對照，而且全部彩圖演出，

編繪遠古、荷西、鄭氏時代、清代、日本時代以及戰後六個時期，

重新勾勒台灣史脈絡與全貌，

更反映各階段台灣人的生活方式與價值觀，

了解台灣，就從這部《認識台灣歷史》開始。

（請沿線對摺，免貼郵票寄回本公司）

新自然主義股份有限公司
THIRD NATURE PUBLISHING CO., LTD.

地址：106 台北市建國南路二段9號10樓之2

Call to Order：886-2-27845369　FAX：886-2-27845358　　劃撥帳號：17239354 新自然主義股份有限公司

E-mail：book@thirdnature.com.tw　　Website：www.thirdnature.com.tw

新自然主義 讀者回函卡

謝謝您購買本書,為加強對讀者的服務並使往後的出書更臻完善,請您詳填本卡各欄,傳真(886-2-27845358)或投入郵筒寄回(免貼郵票),我們將隨時為您提供最新的出版訊息,以及活動相關資料。

書籍名稱:【認識台灣歷史】第_____冊

購買本書的方式:

　　□01在_____市(縣)_____書局購買 □02劃撥 □03贈送
　　□04展覽、演講活動,名稱_____ □05其他_____

您從何處得知本書消息?

　　□01逛書店 □02報紙廣告 □03報紙、雜誌介紹 □04親友推薦 □05書訊
　　□06廣播節目 □07其他_____

您對我們的建議:_____

_____

您的個人資料:姓名_____ 電子信箱:_____

性　　別:□男 □女　出生日期:_____年_____月_____日

電　　話:(　　)_____ 傳　真:(　　)_____

地　　址:□□□_____縣(市)_____鄉鎮區(市)_____路(街)
　　　　　　　　　_____段_____巷_____弄_____號_____樓

教育程度:□01小學 □02國中 □03高中(職) □04大專 □05碩士 □06博士

職　　業:□01學生 □02教育 □03軍警 □04其他公務 □05金融業 □06出版傳播
　　　　　□07醫藥 □08資訊科技 □09法律工作 □10其他自由業 □11其他服務業
　　　　　□12製造業 □13家管 □14其他_____

閱讀嗜好:□身心靈健康 □醫學保健 □本土文化 □漫畫 □原住民 □環保生態 □有機生活
　　　　　□學習成長 □財經商業 □生活百科 □人物傳記 □政治 □法律 □歷史 □宗教

您最常收聽的廣播節目:_____

您最常閱讀的雜誌或報紙:_____